The Making of Beaubourg

By the same author:

LOST NEW YORK

ADHOCISM: THE CASE FOR IMPROVISATION
(with Charles Jencks)

"WHY IS BRITISH ARCHITECTURE SO LOUSY?"
(ed., with Jos Boys)

The Making of Beaubourg

A BUILDING BIOGRAPHY OF THE CENTRE POMPIDOU, PARIS

Nathan Silver

The MIT Press
Cambridge, Massachusetts
London, England

Except for the photo on page 133, which is from the press office of the Centre Pompidou, all photos are by the author.

The texts quoted on pages 132–137 and 140–143, copyright © Ove Arup and Partners, and the text quoted on pages 102–105, copyright © Piano & Rogers, are used by permission.

Chapter 3, "The Winners," was first published in the Spring 1990 issue of *Issues in the Theory and Practice of Architecture, Art and Design,* London.

This book was printed and bound in the United States of America.

Library of Congress Cataloging-in-Publication Data

Silver, Nathan.
    The making of Beaubourg: a building biography of the Centre Pompidou, Paris / Nathan Silver.
        p.   cm.
    Includes index.
    ISBN 0-262-19348-5
    1. Centre Georges Pompidou.   2. Brutalism (Architecture)—France—Paris.
3. Paris (France)—Buildings, structures, etc.   I. Title.
NA6813. F82P3766   1994
725' .8042'0944361—dc20   93-45768
                                                                                  CIP

For Liberty and Gabriel, two of the first million visitors

Contents

Introduction   ix

1   Pompidou's powers   1

2   Where did the design come from?   19

3   The winners   35

4   Setting up in Paris   57

5   The conduct of the job   85

6   Crises, panics, and smooth going   129

7   Toward opening night   156

8   Meaning and influence   173

Appendix: Beaubourg's credits   189

Index   193

The Centre Pompidou, Paris. The building was known as "Beaubourg" until completion, when it received its official name. Designed by Piano & Rogers, Architects; Ove Arup and Partners, Engineers

Introduction

Seven or eight hundred meters north of Nôtre-Dame de Paris is the Centre Nationale d'Art et de Culture Georges Pompidou, more familiarly called the Centre Pompidou—or simply, Beaubourg, which is the name first used, and the name of the place where it stands. It is the work of the architects Piano & Rogers, and the engineers Ove Arup and Partners, winners in 1971 of an international competition set by the President of France. Beaubourg, their design, was accepted by the French government, and was executed over the next five and a half years.

Beaubourg was built to be a mixed-use cultural center, with every level accessible to the public. Underground, there were parking, three public halls, and, slightly separated, an institute for advanced studies in music and acoustics. At ground levels off the street and off a new piazza created at the same time as the building, there were reception and information areas, a children's library and children's workshop, plus the lowest floor spaces of a modern art museum, a library, and an industrial design center.

The first floor was shared by the library, the industrial design center, and general administration. The second floor held the library's main access level and the art museum's administration. The library and museum continued on the third floor, and the museum alone on the fourth floor, where there were some exterior terraces. Finally, the fifth floor was for temporary exhibits, an auditorium for the Cinemathèque Française, a restaurant with bar, and more exterior terraces. Though the allocation of space was thus in the building following its opening in January 1977, the spaces, proportional use, and even the uses themselves were expected to change over the course of time. Beaubourg was designed in particular to be "a live center of information," and in general, to be extremely flexible. Its strategy for internal flexibility is the reason that its structure, public circulation, and mechanical equipment are on the exterior. Partly it is famous just for this: it is the building with its *tripes* outside.

From the time the first designs were shown publicly, Beaubourg was both admired and disliked with passion. It attracted arguments and lawsuits through its construction, and still elicits praise and attacks. Upon opening, it at once became, as foreseen, a principal focus of art and knowledge in France, and, as not entirely foreseen, one of the most popular tourist attractions in Europe. Today it stands as one of the few cultural monuments of the twentieth century that must be reckoned with. If the concept of "monument" has usually reeked of cultural pretension and elitism (a word that itself leapt to life in Paris, 1968), Beaubourg offers a fresh view of what a monument may be. This is not the least of its notable endowments worth pondering.

Since architecture is an art, Beaubourg speaks for itself, and does so eloquently. But there is more of interest about it than the building alone can tell. This includes the original intentions of the client and designers, who they were, how they worked, whom they dealt with, what ideas were in the air at the time, what decisions got left along the way, how architecture in France was practiced, how the fabrication and construction was accomplished, who and what influenced whom or what, and why. Architectural design is not strictly an act; more "a process," as architects are fond of saying to each other—which means that its story is not that of a concept thought up in a designer's bath and carried through just as cleanly, but an unruly gray enterprise. It is a yarn ball of tangled events and decisions with desperate knots, contingent snags, and improvised sections of perhaps entirely different yarn in places, though somehow it all winds on from beginning to end. In retrospect, the gray process of making a building looks barely comprehensible. Usually the participants alone know how the destination was reached, and they don't mind forgetting. Yet the hidden loops and tangles are worth contemplation by others. Architecture is a public art with political, financial, and social considerations that are as natural to its creation as the sheer design and building aspects, and the unraveling leads through the fascinating arrangement of teamwork tasks and incidents, lamely called "administration" or "job management," that orders every building. The process—a presence both abiding and invisible—is as real as the building itself. Beaubourg's invisible procedural arrangements, not durable like steel and glass, were the even larger matters of human intentions and endeavor.

However obvious the attractions of the human story, we seldom attempt to explain how an extraordinary building happened. Usually books on buildings present guides to cultural real estate, pictures of presupposed virtuoso masterworks, or arguments about aesthetic or political controversies. There have been such books already about Beaubourg, and I have not sought to supplant them. My attempted unraveling of the shaggy gray ball of yarn was for the purpose of producing Beaubourg's building biography, for want of a better phrase. As a good human biography offers the procedure of life as an example, I hope Beaubourg's suggests the procedure of a modern building as an example.

As with human biographies, I have organized my narrative to be largely chronological, but some subjects are dealt with topically for simplicity. Most of my story was elicited from files of technical reports prepared by design team leaders; from research in journals, job records, and site records; and from some 30 extended interviews. My desire for brevity where appropriate has accorded with the fact that complete information is never to be had in a process where every decision, argument, and crisis on a building job has many sides to it, the details of which are often forgotten within days. And, though many adventures during the work on Beaubourg were vital and lengthy, design and building operations are essentially similar in pattern, so describing the process doesn't require describing them all.

I regret this book's belated appearance, owing to another tangled process of viscissitudes and delays that needs no telling. When initially completed, my manuscript itself became reference material for other researchers on Beaubourg (one journalist even helped himself to a few of my jokes). At any rate, publication postponement for over a decade hasn't altered the freshness of the participants' early recollections, which I recorded within 18 months of Beaubourg's completion. The delay has also permitted the exclusion of a mass of originally contemplated pictures—to the benefit of the book's price—on the grounds that most readers will now have Beaubourg pictures of their own, and what should be central is the story.

Many people helped and advised me, and I am grateful to them. Most were members of the design team. A few should be thanked by name. A technical file that became an important part of my research was compiled by Peter Hoggett, Alan Stanton, and David Brown. Helen McNeil translated the competition Jury Report for me. The late Peter Rice read the manuscript at several stages and gave me continually constructive advice. Centrally, it was Richard (now Sir Richard) Rogers who first invited me to tackle the book after he read pieces of mine on the building when it opened.

I apologize for the mistakes and anachronisms that must exist. In facts and chronology, sometimes the participants were in disagreement, and in such places I made my own decisions, trying for the right feel. But to be explicator isn't necessarily to be creative only in wrong ways. I have had the pleasure of trying to make others aware of the events, decisions, and cunning behind the building of Beaubourg in order to honor the luster it has, and deserves. As the competition Jury Report said, "Our time loves . . . the boiling-over of life," which was certainly true in the early 1970s, and for this among other reasons I think Beaubourg is the emblematic building of its time. As time has passed, the building's makers—Renzo Piano, Richard Rogers, Peter Rice, Ted Happold, and their creative colleagues—have gone on to design other considerable buildings, and some splendid ones. It isn't unkind to say that none has the uniquely vivacious splendor of Beaubourg.

View toward Montmartre from the southwest emergency stairs, showing the climax of the escalator route—enclosed within a glazed tube—and the piazza below. As anticipated by the designers, Beaubourg's external escalator ride, with its unique diagonal ascent above the horizon of Paris rooftops, is a major attraction for visitors

1 Pompidou's powers

For a building devised to be a triumphant crystallization of the national cultural spirit, Beaubourg's origins lie obscurely in the upheaval of old Paris, with culture no part of the issue. In the 1930s, about seven and a half acres of old housing were cleared at the edge of the Marais district. They were in the center of Paris, where Boccaccio and Pascal had once lived, though the neighborhood had become an area of prostitution with one of the highest tuberculosis rates in France. The forbidding expanse of the Plateau Beaubourg, as it was called, remained for many years. It came to be used as a huge parking lot for trucks serving the food markets at Les Halles, a few hundred yards to the west.

In the 1960s, French government planners decided to move the neighboring Les Halles food markets to the suburb of Rungis. But controversy arose over the future of the market structures. These were a collection of fine, historically important cast-iron and glass pavilions, designed in 1853 by Victor Baltard. In order to save them, it was proposed that some of Paris's needy cultural institutions should be their new occupants. There was a strong claim for a more adequate modern art museum than the Musée National d'Art Moderne, then an ugly building inconveniently located at the Palais de Chaillot, to help restore Paris as the center of the visual arts. Another demand was for a decent public library. France had never had a national movement in the nineteenth or early twentieth centuries to create them as had some other countries, and Paris lacked any large, free, general-purpose library. These cultural claims focused attention on the entire neglected Marais district.

The concept of a library in particular had widespread support, but at first, popular pressure concentrated on the fight to save Baltard's structures in Les Halles. Then, toward the end of 1968, the Bibliothèque des Halles controversy was settled—suddenly, as controversies in Paris tended to be in that year of upheaval. The de Gaulle government announced that the nearby site of Plateau Beaubourg, the parking lot, would be where the Bibliothèque would go, rather than Les Halles. But what sort of library, and backed by whom? Slightly over a year later, the new president, Georges Pompidou, decided to personally adopt the Beaubourg project. He decided it should be both a library *and* a center for the contemporary arts, to include also some better premises for the national modern art museum. So the mixed-use library-plus-arts-center concept for Beaubourg was born, in December 1969, and on the authority of the president.

Pompidou's decision was an outcome of the power held by presidents of France in matters of this sort—and not only in the new Fifth Republic. Since the First Empire of Napoleon, it had been national policy that Paris was more significant than a mere city. It was the heart of the French state. In 1969 Paris had no mayor, or any other directly elected chief municipal executive, only an elected city council. For all major questions of urban policy including town planning and arts patronage, the city council required approval of the Paris préfect, the Council of Ministers of the Republic, and finally the president. Paris, unlike London or New York (but a bit like Washington, D.C.), was run firmly by the state, which as a matter of right and duty had to fully consider the urban affairs of the metropolis in national and international contexts. This was plainly how Président Pompidou perceived Beaubourg. So when official announcements said

> On December 11, 1969, the French President decided to have a Centre erected in the Heart of Paris, not far from Les Halles, devoted to the contemporary arts...

it was true that *the French president had decided*, as few other heads of state in democracies could. Georges Pompidou, an academic turned politician, or, as he was frequently called, de Gaulle's "dauphin," decided things in Paris—not a committee, a Commune, the arts establishment, or the electorate.

The mood of those days was as important as the mood of the president. The May Events of Paris 1968 (like the British National Strike, or America's withdrawal from Vietnam) were a supreme national crisis that led to utter changes in self-appraisal and self-confidence. Everyone feared the very worst, but while French hearts and souls were tested in 1968, the body politic came out miraculously unharmed, and the unforeseeable national salvation generated euphoria. Societal attitudes in arrears are not easy to discern properly because yesterday's Zeitgeist is an extinct beast. Yet many Frenchmen have recorded feeling a sense of great providential release in the first few years after the May Events. Political centrists in particular (such as members of the Gaullist party) believed that their good management and common sense had been tested and proven.

Inspired by its good luck, the French national psyche became confident, and newly daring. France wanted to work with Britain to build the Concorde supersonic commercial plane, and had ambitions to get started with a Channel tunnel. The La Défense business center in Paris, reckoned to compete with the best Europe had to offer, was planned, as was a new airport for Paris, later named the Charles de Gaulle. These were all projects that anti-Gaullists called "elitist monuments"; nevertheless, economic development and European unity were subjects of discussion and enthusiasm through much of French society. Perhaps (as the Situationists of Paris 1968 had demonstrated) even spontaneity could be institutionalized! If the May Events were a vital force, surprisingly benign but regrettably *unfocused,* why not build the magnificent, monumental focus?

This was the background. The way the piazza of the Centre Pompidou looks today with its fire-eaters, mimes, spontaneous gatherings, street theater, and hawkers is, in one sense, an organized, focused version of the more truly ad hoc (and frightening) groupings and events of 1968. While it would be glib to say that the Centre Pompidou was fashioned or even conceived through the psychic requirements of France at that moment, there is no doubt it arose in a singularly euphoric and receptive critical climate. In the mood of those days, Georges Pompidou, the arts lover, the autocrat (as French presidents in the Fifth Republic might be), the European, the cultural federalist, decided also how Beaubourg should be designed. He thought the French government should simply choose the best of the entries in an international architectural competition.

· · · · · ·

Elsewhere, the two firms that were to win the competition were going their decidedly different ways. Piano & Rogers, the architects, were based both in Genoa, and in London in an added-on rooftop office. Some of their past designs had won awards, but they were young, hungry, and short of work. Their professional staff numbered five in Genoa and six in London.

Ove Arup and Partners, the engineers, worked from a number of offices in central London, and indeed outside London. Their headquarters were then (as now) at 13 Fitzroy Street, W1. They were then (as now) one of the biggest firms of consulting engineers in the world. Not at all short of work, the Arup practice was preoccupied with some of the most impressive structural and civil engineering projects of the day, including two vast enterprises in Saudi Arabia and the structure for the Sydney Opera House.

The major participants at Piano & Rogers were—naturally, considering its size—its principals. Renzo Piano (born 1937), a Genoese trained at the Milan Polytechnic, had recently joined with the London group. He maintained residence in Genoa so the practice could be kept binational. Piano's interests lay in rational, technological architecture and construction. He didn't consider himself exclusively an architect but also an industrial designer and a process analyst. Systems of design preoccupied him, and his design showed an unforced architectural lyricism deriving naturally from the closest correspondence to users' needs that could be arrived at. In Italy he had been designing a building in Harrisburg, Pennsylvania, for Olivetti, a corporate client with especially advanced attitudes. Piano was also doing an Italian industry pavilion for Expo 70 in Osaka. Traveling to one of his distant sites in 1968 or 1969, Piano had met Rogers in London, when a doctor friend said he was going to visit a Rogers child who was sick with measles. "Why not come along?" he said. "Rogers is a good architect, a nice fellow, and speaks Italian."

Richard Rogers (born 1933) is English, but from a mainly Italian family. His cousin, the architect Ernesto Rogers, was a teacher of Piano's in Milan. Rogers trained at the Architectural Association School of Architecture in London and then served in the army. When discharged, he became a Fulbright Scholar and went to the Yale School of Architecture for his master's degree. Yale taught him discipline and the capacity for developing strong feelings about a design. At Yale Rogers met his first wife, Su, and his first partner, Norman Foster, both English too. Though Su's training was in sociology, she joined Rogers in the new firm they began back in England. With Norman and Wendy Foster, they became Team 4; later the name of their practice changed to Richard and Su Rogers when work faltered and the Fosters went their own way. John Young and Marco Goldschmied were younger members of the firm who later became partners.

Through the succession of Rogers collaborations, the team members had, like Piano, been conceptually interested in function, design economy, and advanced technology. They commenced their practice in England with some simple houses integrated with the landscape, and then developed some basic but elegant factories, such as the Reliance Controls Factory, Swindon; two for Universal Oil Products, including a fragrance factory in Tadworth; and a "zip-up" series of energy-conscious buildings with components that could be simply attached, or zipped, together. In the ideology of the practice, bad buildings—for example, sentimental ones—were not just weak, but destructive. The Rogers firm, like some others in the vanguard of their profession, felt it was upholding not so much an aesthetic position but an ethical one. This squared well with Piano's philosophy, as the work of both showed. They were uncompromised functionalists and modernists. They were also struggling. In 1970 they decided to share the "no-work situation" by forming a new partnership.

Ove Arup and Partners was an extreme contrast to Piano & Rogers. A well-developed administration was a natural concomitant of its size, and the building of its own administrative structure was one of the most impressive works of the firm. In the early days after its establishment in 1946 in England, the principal interests of the small practice were in structural and civil engineering, but the firm grew to provide complete engineering design services, building economics, and even architecture in a parallel practice, employing thousands in offices worldwide. In 1970, the importance of Ove Arup and Partners was not just that it had designed good footbridges for the Festival of Britain but that the nature of the firm enhanced and encouraged talent. Despite its size, the Arup managerial setup—a model of the best sort of Danish-English liberalism, as a somewhat chauvinistic client put it—tried to be a proper meritocracy, which is how young engineers like Peter Rice and Lennart Grut, later key members of the Beaubourg team, came up fast.

Structures 3 was then one of four divisions of the structural activities of the firm, together with a civil engineering division and the separate architectural practice. Povl Ahm was senior partner of Structures 3, and Edmund Happold was the executive partner. Each division had developed a certain character according to the work it did and the architects associated with it, and Arup's Structures 3 was regarded by some as the most interesting, with-it group. Probably that was because the division worked with some clever architects such as Frei Otto, for example—the German promulgator of exciting tensile structures. Structures 3 was the group then building a competition-winning conference hall in Riyadh, and a mosque in Mecca. The divisions were almost firms within a firm. Division heads had nearly autonomous authority to take on what they could and handle it as they wished, which suited the sense of independence of Happold and others. The division's leading structural engineer for design was Peter Rice. Rice had trained at Belfast, Imperial College London, and Cornell; he had just returned from Australia, where he was site engineer for the Sydney Opera House, to become codirector of Structures 3 with Happold.

· · · · · ·

Back in Paris in December 1969, Président Pompidou considered the best way of initiating the international competition for his culture center, and he decided that the French Ministry of Culture's services should be avoided. Possibly the president believed his ministry would not be quick enough in developing a brief for the design; perhaps he thought it was too set in its ways (or too well informed) to fully adhere to his instructions. Whatever his reservations, Pompidou set up an ad hoc working party that would devise the building's requirements, with Sébastien Loste, a non–Ministry of Culture civil servant, as interim head. Loste recruited François Lombard, a young architect-engineer who had already prepared programs of several buildings for the ministry. A clever technocrat who looked the part, Lombard seemed what the president had ordered, and though he was only 30, he joined the working party as program writer.

What was this "brief," "program," or "programme" (to use the British spelling)? In physical planning, these names denote the bill of particulars, the description of needs—often with proposed floor areas—that elicit an architectural solution. Able homeowners or company managers might be capable of writing a reasonable architectural program for their own activities, but taking command of the requirements for a multitude of interlocking, overlapping, evolving, or conflicting activities is more complicated—especially if the job also includes defining priorities and playing down some of the desirable choices while favoring others. Architects are trained to investigate needs, so it is not unusual for a program to be prepared entirely by the architect, with the client's concurrence. Other times architects work together with clients to determine their programs; sophisticated clients may decide to draw up their needs on their own. Far less usual is for a program to be prepared by a third party. With the approval of the president and Sébastien Loste, that is what Lombard set about doing, armed with a personal definition of his professional work: "Programming is the correspondence between social organization and space organization." A competition doesn't have the winning architect on hand before it is held, so Lombard couldn't seek advice, and later, he knew, the winner would need to be kept on course. Lombard engaged a small staff and hoped he would play a governing role to the end, given the right conditions.

Maintaining independence from the Ministry of Culture was proving to be a good plan. The ministry had reached great heights when Malraux was minister under de Gaulle, building *Maisons de la Culture* in six or seven provincial towns like Grenoble and Amiens. These were a characteristic early 1960s-style idea: performing arts centers such as London's South Bank or New York's Lincoln Center were prime civic objectives of the time, especially in the provinces of France. But they were not what

Pompidou seemed to be looking for at the end of 1969. Loste and Lombard realized that their responsibility was more than just setting down a presidential shopping list. The content was to be very much at the discretion of the *programmation* team, subject only to the president's review and what muffled criticism might emerge afterward from the ministry. They could create the Beaubourg concept; though, finally, they had no authority—that remained with Pompidou.

Two central ideas came directly from Président Pompidou: to hold an international competition, and to build a museum. The programmation team checked with the Ministry of Culture for their evaluation of space demanded by cultural bodies that might deserve consideration. The demand for a library, long called for by the public and press, was fairly obvious. An industrial design center was an idea the programmation team brought forward themselves, because the notion seemed interesting to them: a new institution "combining different forms of art." And for the whole center to function as a concentration of cultural information seemed obvious too, since what was created would be at least a public reading room/book stack/exhibition center/activity base/tourist attraction. The Malraux Maisons de la Culture were monumental piles, generally having over 250,000 square feet of floor area each, but the programmation team was getting even more down on paper than a super Maison de la Culture for Paris. The content alone—a mixture of cultural uses not to be curtailed daily by the short hours associated with performances (since performing arts were not catered for)—seemed set to protect the scheme from the dreaded planning disease Lombard called "Lincoln Centeritis": liveliness for two and a half hours per evening, lifelessness the rest of the time. With a heterogeneous mix for Paris in one superbuilding, the programmation team

hoped to thoroughly integrate the new Centre du Plateau
Beaubourg (as it was at first to be called) from ten in the morning
until midnight.

Lombard was put in touch with young people like himself:
Germain Viatte from the museum, François Barré of the design
center. Bernard Schulz, from the library, was older. What they had
in common was the wish to link artistic expression with everyday
social and economic life. Pompidou, however, kept referring to the
project as a museum. Lombard was apprehensive. Would what
they were doing be appreciated by the president? Programmation
was trying hard to be more than a post office that accepted and
delivered the demands of others. And the documents were piling
up: position papers that argued each case, showing where the
needs seemed to lie. Finally the president was sent the draft
program. His comments came back. Pompidou thought they had
specified not enough parking places, and not enough toilets.
Otherwise, silence was consent.

In July 1970, Président Pompidou accepted the brief prepared by
the programmation team, and the competition became a reality.
The team requested a project manager since Loste's job was done.
Besides, jealousies were already arising. These tensions were
hardly surprising in an administrative structure as complex and
concerned with precedent as the civil service (which the working
party of course was part of), but they seemed to provide a warning
of the strains that would be exacerbated once the public at large
had an actual design to criticize, a construction site to contend
with, and public expenditure to oppose. Single-mindedness and
diplomacy would be required; for Pompidou, the Ministry of
Culture still didn't seem to have the right qualities. Lombard
wrote a job description to delineate the project manager they
ought to be seeking, including a helpful profile of the ideal

candidate. Youngish; with broad construction background; perhaps with some experience of working for a cultural institution. . . . Pompidou ignored all this and appointed Robert Bordaz, who was elderly and had no professional knowledge of construction. On the other hand, Bordaz was a *Conseiller d'État*, a senior civil servant of the highest caliber. He was an intellectual who contributed to literary magazines and helped to run the Cannes Film Festival. At one stage of his career he had been in charge of the ORTF, the French broadcasting authority. During the Indochinese war, he had engineered the French evacuation after Dienbienphu. In construction management, he had been responsible for a French exhibition in Moscow, but he had had only one reasonably demanding job: taking charge of the French national pavilion in Montreal at Expo 67.

Despite Bordaz's unsuitability to their profile, the programmation team quickly conceded that he should be just right. He was a recognized master of political administration and diplomacy. Although he was scarcely known to the public, he commanded great respect from politicians and other civil servants. Pompidou appreciated his flexibility, understanding, and ability to bring pressure to bear, and the president evidently expected those qualities to be necessary. At Bordaz's age, this was likely to be his final assignment before retirement.

Bordaz took on the job by first formalizing the tasks and assignments. The ad hoc programmation team became part of a new *Délégation*, later to be called the *Établissement Public*. This confirmed the Centre Beaubourg project as administratively independent, at least, from the ministries. Lombard was reappointed—he was the only one who spoke English, which later was to prove important. Other posts were envisaged for a head of administrative staff (filled by Claude Mollard about a year later), and a head of construction control (at first Robert Regard, later

Lombard briefly, then André Darlot). The client structure of the Centre Beaubourg thus arose quickly and neatly after Bordaz's appointment—he was certainly good at administration. Would Bordaz be as good at managing the selection, design, and construction of the physical structure?

. . . . . .

In London early in 1971, Ted Happold, executive partner at Arup in charge of Structures 3, read an announcement in the Royal Institute of British Architects' (RIBA's) *Competition News* that an international competition for a cultural center in Paris was to be held. With his own cash, Happold sent off a bank check for 200 francs, which was the cost of the design program, refundable to applicants who made an acceptable entry. While he waited for his competition kit from the *Délégation pour la realisation du Centre du Plateau Beaubourg*, he considered one of the conditions of the competition: participation was open only to architects or teams directed by an architect, as defined and recognized by the International Union of Architects.

Of course, Structures 3 worked with many eminent architects. The Piano & Rogers office, though well published, wasn't very eminent. But Happold remembered the Rogerses as being talented and congenial. The way they had met was that the Rogers office about a year before—and before the merger with Piano— had been asked by a corporate consulting firm called Wolff Olins to help make a presentation to the Chelsea Football Club. Wolff Olins was to concentrate on Chelsea's image and appeal, and the Rogers office was to design a new grandstand for the football ground. Never one to settle for second best, Richard Rogers wrote to Frei Otto in Germany asking him if he would be consultant for the grandstand's engineering. Even at that time Otto probably had enough work to keep him busy for the next twenty years. He recommended Happold and Structures 3 at Arup. Like many such ventures, the Chelsea football stand didn't come off—not for lack of brilliance in the design, a totally openable-closable structure, but because (Rogers later said) the presentation got bogged down in sweatshirts, hamburger vending wrappers, and Chelsea football rattles.

Yet the Rogers office had been stimulating to work with. Happold and his administrative associates Gerry Clarke and Michael Barclay discussed the Beaubourg competition at length, and finally decided to try to lure in Richard and Su Rogers. Peter Rice, Happold's structural designer colleague, was back from his latest project. Happold rang the Rogerses, found they had become Piano & Rogers, and he and Rice went to their offices for lunch to put the question.

All parties knew that competitions are dicey propositions. The history of success in international architectural competitions is daunting. Entrants may never properly fathom the taste and influence of some cranky dilettante judge from Uruguay, who may team up with a town planner from Bulgaria and deny prizes to the deserving. And deserving by what standards? Then, the sheer number of entries in important competitions (500 is common; there were to be 681 in Paris) makes success a bit like a lottery result. Finally, even to win is not to guarantee one's honored presence at an eventual ribbon-cutting ceremony. This can be thwarted by the client's cold feet (as in the 1968 Amsterdam City Hall competition), or perhaps by a runner-up being asked to build a design, usually for suspected reasons of crass chauvinism and intrigue (cf. an international competition in 1969, about a year before the Beaubourg competition, in Austria[1]).

---

1 Sponsored by the Austrian Republic and the City of Vienna, this competition was for a national

If they were to enter, a lot of things had to be taken into account. First, the timing. Happold argued that this was perfect for them as a group. The Burrell Gallery competition for Glasgow had just been held, open to all Commonwealth architects, which had exhausted most of their fellow British, Australian, and Canadian competition-enterers (and Piano & Rogers: they had entered but the results hadn't been announced. Later they learned that they hadn't even been placed). Then had come the Parliamentary office building for London, exhausting most of the rest of the British architects (Happold's team helped the architects who were eventually placed second; Piano & Rogers hadn't entered). Rice, sitting quietly, was described by Happold as the perfect design engineer in structures—a man of immense talent. But working on a design for France might prove difficult, someone said.

Su Rogers didn't believe it. She thought France could be a good place to work. At least the French respected creativity. Renzo Piano, who was present too, very much agreed. He thought the winning solution should stand a fair chance of getting built, because in France a matter like that would not get hung up in partisan legislative battles, it could just be decreed by the president. But Richard Rogers kept coming up with all the reasons why they shouldn't enter. The London office was fully occupied for the moment on a scheme for a shopping center in Cambridge. The Paris competition program seemed very political to him: why this supercenter? Should there be such a concentrated and centralized building for the arts? Wouldn't it be elitist? Besides, though the prize-giving jury had a few impressive names, which ones would prevail?

---

conference center and UN offices. The Building Design Partnership of London won first prize. The sponsors then decided to hold a second competition among the top four places. Cesar Pelli of the USA won this. The job was then given to the Austrian firm that had secured second place in the second competition.

John Young, contributing to a Piano & Rogers project for the first time as a partner, had joined the discussion. The comments he heard were still mainly negative. Would it be a fair competition? The RIBA had given ambivalent advice to its membership about entering. And after the Burrell competition, their own practice seemed far too short of money to risk more on another. Only a few months before, a providential financial relationship had ended: "Richard and Su Rogers in association with DRU." Design Research Unit, an industrial design firm, had staked the office and paid salaries in return for all eventual profit. (If DRU hadn't chosen to call off the arrangement just then, they might have had control of all Beaubourg's fees, something over £2,000,000 to the architects alone!)

Su had to leave for another meeting. To everyone's surprise after all the cold water, she got up and said, "If Ted says we should do it, I say we should, too." Richard decided he would agree with his wife on that, but only if money for expenses was forthcoming. Rice and Happold went away and, on their own authority out of their divisional budget at Arup, allocated about £300 as a contribution toward drafting costs.

Renzo Piano was optimistic. He and the Rogerses had already begun to work on a number of experimental projects including ARAM, a prefab hospital design for Third World countries. At least the team's competition design should end up in the top 30, he thought, each of which was designated to receive an honorarium of 10,000 francs. Once it had been agreed that they should enter, Richard Rogers became more positive—at least competitions were experiences in research and in working together. He asked Piano to find the manpower. Piano took on the task, trying to inveigle first one, then another skilled architectural assistant. His third and usually busiest choice was Gianni Franchini, whom Piano had known at architectural school and who had worked for him before.

Piano decided that if Franchini was away or unavailable, he would give up. But Franchini was in, and was available. When he heard the proposition, he said he was willing to work on the entry as much as they wanted. So it was settled that the *Centre du Plateau Beaubourg* competition would be entered by the group after all. The determining factors were fixed largely by chance, but they were going to participate.

Part of the east
elevation. Having the
building's guts outside
increased the problems
of weather damage and
water staining, but it
simplified fire safety,
maintenance, and
replaceability

2   Where did the design come from?

In the development of the Piano & Rogers–Arup Beaubourg competition design, the participants entered, naturally enough, with certain mental baggage of theory about architecture, the preoccupations that stirred them at the time, and notions that were generally in the air. But firm attitudes and predispositions don't always lead on to rigid forms. More than most buildings— more, perhaps, than any before—the Centre Pompidou was to evolve in the fashioning. Was this because improvisation came to the rescue of earlier improvidence? That is what improvisation is for, sometimes, but evidently not in this case.

Another way to use improvisation is as a strong, informing discipline from the beginning, in order to deliberately postpone decisions and maintain flexibility. A loose framework such as this isn't necessarily a concept lacking in vigor. For example, one early notion of the team was that nearly everything in a building like

Beaubourg should be subject to easy replacement. For the designers to follow that through seriously in the event they won would mean their needing to impose the burden of reversibility on nearly every construction operation. Ultimately, a design like that would probably be more costly, and perhaps three times more arduous in accomplishment, than other designs. Their technique of improvisation at this stage was to flirt with the reversibility concept, rather than pounce on it, until it could be settled into a full strategy of flexibility for building replacements, if that was what was finally decided.

Piano, Richard Rogers, Happold, Rice, John Young, Franchini, and to a lesser extent Marco Goldschmied and Su Rogers set about designing through "brainstorming" cerebration sessions, where pet notions like replaceability of parts were paraded and argued about. It was far from a free range of ideas. They knew more or less what they wanted. In a profession full of versatile practitioners who could turn out office slabs looking like Chicago Revisited one month and tourist hotels looking like tropical villages the next, Piano & Rogers had peculiarly settled if not fixed views, and these governed their search for creative resources.

Some conceptual prototypes for Piano were buildings he had done in Italy since 1965. His interest in lightweight shells had expanded to include industrial building design where elements, and even the machines for making them, were designed by Piano—often in conjunction with the factory run by his brother. There was a laboratory he designed in Genoa, 1968, whose roof was a lightweight framework of steel tetrahedrons, with lightweight precast concrete grade beams for foundations; and an Olivetti plant in Scarmagno he designed the same year, with a roof system of fiberglass and acrylic unboltable elements. The

Rogerses' thought processes embraced such accomplishments as their Reliance controls factory in Swindon, first stage 1967; it had been completed in ten months using available construction subsystems, yet with simplicity and flexibility—qualities not always associated with readily available components. They liked to use lightweight industrial materials, and were influenced by late 1960s theories of social change to believe that change was perpetual. All Piano's and the Rogerses' previous designs had developed from particular individual programs, as is generally the case. But looking back at them, one notices that, in purely formal terms, the work of both during this period almost always showed plain rectangular plans with frequent internal complexities (the Zip-Up House plan 1969, the Osaka Italian Industry Pavilion 1969, among others). Their design predilection for responsive, "custom" forms within and about a serenely ruling rectilinear space was to emerge again in a big way.

The Piano & Rogers office admired advanced technology, a stance that might appear to have come from man-made America. But it went beyond any interest shown by architects in America (who as a rule are more mistrustful of technology). Coming from non-Americans, the seemingly hyper-American faith in technology was ultimately to turn out particularly well. Other examples where ardent but distant admiration perpetuated higher achievement include the Maison Carrée in Nimes, far from Rome, which has been called the ideal Roman architectural form, and Nehru, who is sometimes called the perfect English gentleman. Distant appreciation is known to lend undistracted, if sometimes romantic, conviction. Yet the Piano & Rogers office wasn't hyper-American or necessarily romantic. Its pure faith in this particular kind of modernism was, perhaps, the buildable expression of the

architects' unflinching belief in rational design as the only secure
guiding principle in the deployment of material and artistic
resources. Rational design! A contradiction in terms, many
American architects would have said in 1970. Or perhaps an
oxymoronic joke. The Piano & Rogers team still believed the
machine age could humanely work. A long 50 or 60 years after the
modern movement began, they considered that architects still had
a right to suppose that invention, resourcefulness, and reason were
the proper sources of architectural beauty, or (the ethic rather than
the aesthetic), truth. Above all, what a thing was, was how it
should look; nuts, bolts, budget, fire regulations. This kitchen-
sink working philosophy was certainly not unique to Piano &
Rogers, but it had been far more widely shared among architects a
generation earlier, before disenchantment with what had been
known as "functionalism" had set in. For Piano, the Rogerses, and
their colleagues, to return home too soon in the voyage of
functionalism was fainthearted—there were continents yet to
discover.

The Beaubourg official program they studied was succinct at
heart. Like most competition briefs, it was (deceptively) merely a
matter of getting sums right, arranging ideas. In gross areas, it
called for the following:

		Interior Spaces (m2)	Open-air Spaces (m2)
(A)	RECEPTION. ORIENTATION.		
	(A1) Entrance-Reception (suggested area)	3,000	
	(A2) Reception for children	400	300
	(A3) Cafeteria, Canteen	1,000	400
	(A4) Restaurant	900	300
		5,300	1,000

(B)   MAIN ACTIVITIES.

(B1) Current Events Room	1,000	
(B2) Industrial Design: Permanent Gallery and Documentation Service	1,650	
(B3) Experimental Gallery of Contemporary Art	800	1,000
(B4) Temporary Exhibitions	4,000	2,800
(B5) Theaters and Meetings	3,300	
(B6) Museums	15,800	2,000
(B7) Library	15,000	
(B8) Specialized Documentation and Research	3,150	
(B9) Temporary and Permanent Storage	5,500	
	50,200	5,800

(C)   MANAGEMENT.

(C1) Scientific and Administrative Personnel	2,500	200
(C2) Social Services	450	
(C3) Supervision and Control	490	
(C4) Lodgings	860	
(C5) Workshops and Storerooms	2,000	
(C6) Technical Areas	2,500	
	8,800	200
TOTAL (A + B + C)	64,300	7,000

(D)   PARKING.

(D1) Personnel Vehicles	2,500
(D2) Visitors' Vehicles	20,000
(D3) Coaches	1,500
(D4) Trucks	1,000

In addition, some "fundamental considerations" were pointed out in the program. The center had to be easily accessible. "The pedestrian at street level should not be forced to follow a long path towards a special entrance." Also, "The public will enter on all sides." And, "The visitor should be tempted to go everywhere." Obviously the library and the contemporary arts sector would attract different visitors, " . . . one sedentary the other nomad [i.e.]: readers and visitors. If these two groups were to stay separated, the desired effect would be lost." Ultimately,

> Everything is based . . . upon the ease and freedom with which the visitor will share in the Centre's offerings, and the way in which he will be constantly attracted towards them.

Among the "fundamental considerations" was a section on flexibility. This was well thought through in the program, and extremely interesting to the P & R–Arup group. It said, in part,

> The areas given have been estimated [to be] sufficient for the full exercise of all activities presently foreseen. No extension of the building is to be planned, as the collections will be periodically renewed. . . . On the other hand, the Centre's internal flexibility should be as large [i.e., great] as possible. In a living and complex organism such as the Centre, the evolution of needs is to be especially taken into account.

Though flexibility was in the brief, it was unemphatic. But flexibility suddenly seemed the key. The team was seeking it, and, finding it, they raised it high—they had worked on the principle so often before. Flexibility to them meant the opportunity for space without constraint (after all, the word used wasn't mere *adaptability*). At a very early point in the team's brainstorming sessions, they therefore decided to push outside all the interfering things that fill the internal body of buildings. The idea developed simply and logically from there. Push out the structural system—

and the stairs, elevators, pipes—all out, in order to have the maximum possibility of changing use. On one side, push out all the mechanical equipment. On the other, push out all the user circulation and other movements. As Piano described it, "...then we took a decision: are we going to show all this, or cover it with a false facade? That was it. Our design. It was absolutely super-simple."

The simplicity of the notion wasn't unprecedented: for eloquent open spaces, there were the great railroad station sheds and early wrought iron and steel exhibition halls, to start with. Not very long before, the architect Cedric Price in England had proposed an open and flexible "Fun Palace" for the theatrical manager Joan Littlewood, which the Beaubourg team particularly contemplated. And the English Archigram group since the early 1960s had been illustrating fantastic buildings with their guts spectacularly hanging out. All these (and others) were wholesome precedents that didn't provide anything as treacherously snatchable as a bald archetype to copy. They were only information, and as such, they offered both vital and inappropriate data for students to sift through judiciously. So the Piano & Rogers team did.

They also asked themselves, What about this building's urban performance? The area would be blasted by years of construction. It had been a truck parking lot for 40 years. Could they give the space back? A few design team members realized that street theater was very strong in France, and the number of wandering groups in Paris was exceptional. But Paris had few squares of the Italian kind, and indeed, less open ground than any comparable Western city. The team decided to leave about half the site vacant for a "piazza" to help redress this (oddly, this idea was not adopted by many other contestants). The building would be parallel to, and hard against, the main road to protect the public from noise and pollution, and "to keep the street a street," as someone said, strengthening the vista to Nôtre-Dame. On the eastern front along the street, the mechanical equipment of the building could be a continuation of the mechanical movement of road traffic. The western front could continue the movement of people from the piazza up onto the facade—another primary conception. Essentially, the building they were deciding upon would amount to no more than seven (later five) piazzas, stacked above each other. In its flexible performance, well, "...now it's a culture center," Piano said much later; "...after that perhaps an Open University; later on, I don't know. A cattle market?"

There was a populist drift in the team's interpretative planning. What about May 1968, the people, their rightful social demands? To rectify such soppiness, Happold proposed they also do some basic market research on the jury. A way to win a competition might be to think about what the jury wanted. You could "psych them out," which was the expression Happold used. Since everyone has different values, in their ideal competition entry they would need something for everybody.

> When you have sex, religion, and the Royal family, you know you're onto a winner. One guy's going to worry about social benefits and you've got to have it all there. Another guy's going to worry about constructibility and you've got to have a bit for him. And then there's the guy...

Market research on the jury wasn't entirely a joke. The assessing jury was akin to a group of potential customers, and of course an entrant would be wise to think very carefully about what each juror might be looking for—the best theories and principles would be useless if the scheme was only to be glanced at and cast aside. The team had gone through the list of jurors, had thought about them, and had decided that as a group they were pretty unpredictable—in fact, this had been one of Richard Rogers's main arguments against entering. But while they wholeheartedly believed in sheer excellence as the only gambit likely to win, with the larger team assembled they briefly looked at the jury list again:

E. Aillaud, architect. Wasn't known.

Sir Frank Francis. He was head of the British Museum, but no one knew where he stood on architecture (although the BM did have a huge project going with a progressive British architect, Colin St. John Wilson).

P. Johnson, architect. Philip Johnson, the eminent American, had taught the Rogerses at Yale, and they liked and respected him. But they thought he had a fashion-crazy side, and they didn't know which side he would be showing. Potentially, the strongest character in the jury.

M. Laclotte. Wasn't known.

O. Niemeyer, architect. A Brazilian, famous especially for his sculptural concrete roof shells. No one felt especially sympathetic to his work nor expected much rapport with him.

G. Picon. Unknown to the team.

J. Prouvé, architect. Highest rating from Piano, who knew about him. Prouvé was a man devoted to basic technology, and in his career was concerned with prefabrication, rapid assembly, quantity production, and innovative methods in building.

W. Sandberg. The curator of the Stedelijk Museum in Amsterdam, and the most important museum curator of the century, Richard Rogers said (he and Su had met Sandberg through their friend Naum Gabo). The trend toward popularizing great public museums—carpeting them, putting in decent graphics—began with Sandberg. A quite old man.

J. Utzon, architect. Jorn Utzon was a Dane with much respectable

housing work to his credit. Then he won the Sydney Opera House
competition. This seemed a useful link with Arup, and he was very
talented, but how would he react to a quite different design
philosophy? (In the event Utzon became ill, and didn't participate.)

This was the jury. There were few certainties to cling to. On the
whole the members didn't seem actually antipathetic, which was
some consolation. Clearly, what the team had to do was to submit
the best possible design according to their beliefs.

With the basic conception of the building established, some key
details had to be considered. Richard and Su Rogers and Renzo
Piano had also followed this course many times before. If nearly
every plan they had done was a miniplan of the Beaubourg
scheme, some of their other favored attributes were included in
the scheme for Beaubourg's general-purpose spaces too: a plan and
elevation responding only to necessities, lightweight materials,
advanced technology, and prefabrication. The conceptual
particulars streaming into Beaubourg derived also, like plan form,
from long-held preferences. Even the space-frame structural
design that Happold and Rice began to study was related to what
Piano's office in Genoa had been doing recently.

Not that the two engineers from Arup didn't have their own well-
considered structural design intentions. Happold had been
impressed by the magnitude and precision of steelwork in
Buckminster Fuller's geodesic dome built for the United States
pavilion at Expo 67, Montreal (though he had been very
unimpressed at the logic of having the upper struts the same
thickness as the lower ones). And when he visited the construction
site on the Frei Otto Olympic Stadium for Munich, his eyes were
opened to large-scale steel castings, which were being used atop
the masts to hold the roof cables. Steel castings were nineteenth-

century technology brought up to date. Compared to members of rolled steel, they were relatively brittle, but metallurgical science had developed a good deal. The roofs at Mecca and Riyadh that Structures 3 had been working on had steel tensile coverings not dissimilar to those of the Olympic Stadium, so the Arup practice had considerable recent experience in advanced steel structures. For Beaubourg, concrete was a material that never crossed Happold's mind.

Though Rice had spent the previous few years working in concrete, doing thin-shell and other calculations for the Sydney Opera House, he was also aware that steel technology had many new developments that could be applied in buildings. Steel castings were already well exploited in other fields: big elements were used in ship turbines, in sluice gates for dams and power stations, and generally in large mechanical plants. But castings had dropped out of use in the building industry. Rice was keen to try them out at Beaubourg—where the scale and prestige of the job, if it was built, would amply justify the trials, and where they would draw the interest of research-oriented manufacturers.

Providing sketches and ideas for Beaubourg's boxlike envelope, Happold and Rice brainstormed too. They started with the architectural concept, of which they thoroughly approved. Part of their job was to complete one page in the text submitted to the competition jury. They decided there would be space only to describe "an attitude" toward the steelwork—some sort of trenchant approach to the problem that would make the jury realize, without having full details, that the structure too was to be a clear expression of the performance of the building. They said to each other, Let's think of ideas that will give the design the same *esprit* as the Eiffel Tower, or the Gare de Lyon. Using this approach, they eventually decided on tubular steel water-filled columns, tubular struts, diagonal tension ties for bracing, and floor trusses that might need only to be wedged to the columns. What this last notion meant was that the floors could actually be moved up and down, for ultra-flexibility. The analogy for this in their minds was the docks in Barrow-in-Furness, which have twin walls of steel with cranes moving up and down, and ships beneath. Why not a building with its sides performing like that and the floors going up and down? It's just possible we can solve it, thought Happold. It won't be tenable against fire, but it shows our attitude, thought Rice.

An item in the brief that did frighten the Arup engineers, however bold they were ready to be, was the seemingly impossible timetable. Despite the program's saying "the decision of the jury does not imply any inherent right to execution for the prizewinning competitors" (competition briefs always said that), it went on to state as a mandatory requirement "the possibility of realizing the project within the time limits (1973–1974–1975)." What was this? Even assuming it was possible to make an almost immediate start by midsummer 1971, that only allowed a maximum of four and a half years for completion of 95,000 square meters of construction. By whatever measure of the project—time for resolving design complexities, probable time necessary for political and administrative steps to be taken, time needed before delivery of industrial building elements worth multi-millions—this seemed crazy. The competitors thought the big rush showed that the building had to be open before the next election. The engineers felt there should be a clear dissent from this unrealistic timetable, and, at the end of the submission's mandatory text of eight pages, they put one in. If it hadn't been for some friendly help later, this might have sunk the entry.

The design was done partly in London and partly in Genoa, with Piano and Franchini venturing north and Richard Rogers going south, doing the first sketches. Su Rogers barely participated; John Young worked on it a little, Marco Goldschmied not much. Peter Flack, a young assistant, did a lot of the final drawing. Memories vary about how long the work took, but a mean figure is five or six solid weeks for a number of people varying between one and four, over about three months.

The pieces fell into place. Flexible envelope, simple geometrical form, open piazza, occupancy zoned to reinforce integration with the city, high-technology steel structure, exterior mechanical equipment, and building circulation. All members of the team had movement in mind: it goes with change. An analysis of the exacting requirements for underground traffic connections was done by Michael Sargent in Arup's Highways & Bridges Transportation group, and he also helped to solve the parking problems by moving all vehicles underground, as some of the more technical parts of the building were to be. Renzo Piano and Richard Rogers both had an unvanquishable faith in Le Corbusier's idea of a building on *pilotis,* or stilts, with a covered public space underneath and only the smallest of service and lobby links to the ground. This was adopted. The competition design showed a sunken piazza to provide shelter from the wind, and around the edge, basement spaces opened upward to form small shops.

Along with trying to make himself think as the jury might think, Happold sometimes tried to fathom other secrets of success. "Every architectural competition winner has a strong, clear pedestrian circulation system," was one of the precepts he came up with. This concurred with the movement of people that they had already settled on. At that time, the developing competition design showed big rectangular holes opening the nether parking decks to the piazza surface, with an impressive cluster of elevators on the exterior from that central point, and two snaky escalators going both ways across the piazza facade, connecting exterior galleries. On the drawing for the piazza elevation, the diagonally braced structural cage was only about three-fifths filled by building volume. The remainder was shown as terraces and open space potentially available to be filled in, when an equal volume elsewhere got opened up, but meanwhile, all was metal tracery and sky.

Last but not least, information was to be hung on the structure of the facades—news, announcements, shapes, lights, and movements that would be events in their own right. This notion plainly derived from the German architect Oscar Nitzchke (who had taught at Yale at one time, and had worked in Britain). Nitzchke's famous unbuilt 1932–35 *Maison de la Publicité* design for the Champs Élysées had proposed a building with a metal grid facade, actually to be diagonally braced like Beaubourg's, covered with graphic advertisements continuously erected and dismantled with a rooftop crane. That Beaubourg's own electrographic art (if provided) should, unlike Nitzchke's, be of strong social rather than commercial worth, and should respond to its own age and culture in a forceful way, was illustrated by the competition presentation. Beaubourg's main facade drawing showed pictures snipped out of magazine photos and pasted on (a popular late 1960s architectural presentation technique). There were very large heads of Vietnam soldiers wearing helmets; a map of the world in a strip with superimposed grid; mobs of people in two sizes, snipped out of two magazines; then, lettered words saying "A ANIMATED MOVIES PRODUCTION FOR THE"—interrupted by elevator shafts—"COMPUTER TECHNIQUE OF."

Down near the piazza level, much smaller but still in giant letters filling one whole bay, the architects put lettering with the sociopolitically incisive and timely words:

CAROLINE
GO TO KANSAS CITY
IMMEDIATELY
YOUR FRIEND
LINDA HAS BEEN
BUSTED

On galleries and escalators, scores of people were shown, ostensibly looking down on the people at piazza level. Piazza crowds were ostensibly looking up. The design proposition was two planes at right angles, disposed so they would be visually on offer to each other: people-movement and programmed information on the facade; people-movement and unprogrammed activities on the piazza. This to the team seemed a logical manifestation to have developed out of the competition program, which said plenty about involvement, mixing, and close contact, but didn't indicate how this could work, or to what end. Richard Rogers took home the program, and a couple of days later he came back with a draft for the submission text, the required blurb explaining the design concepts. The first words, which several jurors afterwards admitted struck them very much, were, "We recommend that the Plateau Beaubourg is developed as a 'Live Centre of Information' covering Paris and beyond."

The "tertiary steel" structure supporting the external escalators. In the detailed design of the structure, the tertiary steel was made to connect to the primary structure with adaptable fixings so different arrangements of external elements could be accommodated in the future

3   The winners

The final date for submission of the Beaubourg competition entries was June 15, 1971, the postmark being the evidence for mailed entries. Even mailed entries had to be at the competition office in Paris no later than midnight the 24th of June. Piano & Rogers followed a last-minute rush schedule.

It is a traditional work pattern of the profession that architectural concepts are explored until the last possible moment, leaving open as many options as possible for as long as possible. Finally the scheme is "frozen." Then there is a big rush to complete the graphic presentation, very late nights, the laying on of extra help, and the work is frantically completed *en charette*—a phrase originally referring to the cart that conveyed architectural drawings to the venerable École des Beaux-Arts of Paris, where much work en charette obviously happened. The P & R–Arup Beaubourg team was en charette in London through the evening of the 15th of June; then Marco Goldschmied took the tube of rolled-up drawings to what was then a 24-hour post office near Trafalgar Square, arriving an hour or so before midnight. And there the tube was measured. And there it was declared too long. It couldn't be mailed.

It was too late to do anything about it except what Goldschmied did: he borrowed scissors, cut down the tube, and cut a strip off each of the presentation drawings, which had been designed to fit together in a horizontal and vertical mosaic. (When told all this later, the juror Philip Johnson said, "I wondered what happened. It all looked a little too casual.") The package was then accepted, stamped, and the stamps were cancelled. Goldschmied paid the man in the little window and left.

Four mornings later, like the corpse in *Les Diaboliques,* the tube returned horribly from the beyond. It was found lying on Richard Rogers's desk when he came in, stamped "Insufficient Postage." In a fury, Rogers tore down to the post office with it. He insisted it was all the post office's fault, the tube had been improperly weighed by them, and he demanded that it be sent with postmarks on the new stamps showing a date no later than the 15th of June. But apparently one of the most sanctified principles of London post office procedure is correct postmarking, and to backdate a postmark is inconceivable. Rogers's shouting and threatening wasn't doing much good, so he started wheedling. At last a compromise was agreed involving a cancellation smudged while backs were turned. To Rogers's grudging satisfaction, the dreaded tube was on its way again.

But apparently not for long. A few days further on, the French Embassy in London phoned the architects' office to ask if they had completed and sent off their entry. Evidently none of the English entries had arrived in Paris. Panic again! But it seemed more odd than sinister, since Piano & Rogers knew that its entry, at least, hadn't gone off with the rest. Ruth Elias, a young American helping out in the office, spoke on the phone to Richard who was teaching for a few days in the south of England: should they send another set of prints as requested? Money was very low. With his bad-luck scene at the post office doubtless still in mind, Richard said, "Ruthie, it's a loser. We've had the benefit. Forget it."

Rogers's nonhubristic attitude in his final trial must have pleased the gods, because they were finally assuaged. The drawings had indeed arrived, as had all the other English entries. They had been put in some room and temporarily forgotten. After that, not much time passed before the momentous news arrived. Piano phoned London from Genoa a few weeks later to say that they had won, and they were being asked to go to Paris at once. It was an incredible shock. The few people hanging about in the London office were amazed, and beside themselves with excitement.

But just finding key members of the design team was a problem. For one thing, there had been a personal event of some magnitude going on: Richard and Su Rogers were splitting up. After some trial separations, they decided that Richard would move out and get his own flat with Ruth Elias (today Lady Rogers—the second Mrs. Richard Rogers), but as far as the office knew, details weren't all settled. Other people were on a long summer weekend.

Rogers was flabbergasted at the news when he received it somewhere outside London. He phoned Ruth Elias twice, the first time saying they had won the competition. And the second, after phoning Paris, to say, We're going to Paris this afternoon. Meanwhile, word was spreading. The entire small staff of Piano & Rogers in London enthusiastically decided to make the trip. As John Young said later, they had to pinch themselves to believe it was true: they had no work, and indeed there had been no particular reason to go into the office, so little was there to do. Now they could forget all that. After years of struggle looking after their chronic invalid of an architectural practice, the invalid had suddenly had a complete remission and was ready to dance around the bed.

. . . . . .

In Paris about ten days before, on the 5th of July, the Beaubourg competition jury had convened to do its work. Jorn Utzon had sent word that he couldn't attend for reasons of health. The jury thereupon appointed one of the substitutes, Herman Liebaers, director of the Royal Library of Belgium. His being an eminent foreigner seemed more important than his not being an architect (the other available substitute was a French architect). Jean Prouvé acted as president of the jury; Gaëtan Picon, whose credits were unknown to the P & R–Arup team—actually, he was a prominent French writer, cultural figure, and academician—was vice president. Another person unidentified by the winning team took his seat: Michel Laclotte, head curator of the Department of Painting, the Louvre. All jury members were either architects or else represented fields of interest provided for in the Beaubourg designs. The prospective users themselves were not on the jury, to avoid the suspicion of any distortions. Robert Regard, secretary-general of the Délégation, represented the technical commission and programming group as professional adviser.

First the jury decided on how to decide. They looked at the basic points that had to be covered within the competitors' texts and promulgated criteria as follows:

- the general spirit: an architectural translation of the center's philosophy

- "insertion" into the urban environment (a welcoming, congenial sort of architecture was to be looked for)

- the closest possible unity of form and function

- flexibility

- access and circulation (the encouragement of pedestrians in particular)

- public reception (in common, and for each activity)

- the scheme's agreement with the program

- communications (the word used, *liasons,* was not amplified further in the Jury Report)

- the technical conception (safety, control, structure, mechanical equipment)

- principles of construction (likely delays were to be taken into account)

As it transpired, the jury took particular account of architectural quality, flexibility of spaces, and the potential communicative relations between the building and its surroundings.

There were 681 valid submissions as checked by the Délégation. These were made anonymous through a double control of numbers, like two keys for a safe (though of course an idiosyncratic presentation style might always be discerned through any number of barriers, and a juror might know that a friend was entering with a certain scheme). For their working method, the jury decided that mornings would be devoted to individual examinations of the projects. Each juror marked schemes with "A," meaning he very strongly recommended it, "+," meaning he was taking a fairly positive view, "-," meaning a fairly negative view, and "N," meaning he was strongly against. Afternoons were devoted to a mutual examination of projects marked "A" or "+," and only one "A" or "+" vote would get a scheme looked at by everyone.

For the first three days the jury didn't make any final selections. At the end of that stage they had about 100 entries that stood out over the rest. In the second stage, they reexamined 40 to 60 of those, discarding many, but also bringing back a few that seemed particularly good according to the technical requirements. By a third stage the jury felt that, in conscience, they hadn't eliminated anything of interest in accordance with their criteria. They reexamined each remaining scheme, taking note of the professional adviser's technical remarks before they rejected one. No revelations arose in this phase, they commented—it simply allowed them to retain a few supplementary schemes.

In a fourth stage, the jury asked the professional adviser and experts in his group for their views on the 60 remaining projects. The comments were given to the jury in full session. Finally, after a visit to the site and the district, each juror expressed himself on the projects worthy of at least receiving mention.

On the 15th of July, the jury decided that they should award only one prize (as was their privilege under the competition rules) and should give all the prize money of 250,000 francs to the first place. The choice of the winner was elected by a count of eight to one. The name of the dissenter was not recorded, but P & R was later privately told that it was "one of the French architects." The vote was in favor of project 493, which soon proved to be by Messrs. Piano, Rogers, Franchini, Architects; Ove Arup and Partners, Consultant Engineers. (The error that promoted Franchini, employed as an assistant, over Su Rogers and John Young, who were omitted principals of the practice, was a bit of last-minute submission sloppiness that was never completely corrected in the annals of the competition.) The jury chose 30 other finalists who were each to receive 10,000 francs in accordance with the rules. They also decided, unanimously, to give a special mention to project 641 because of its great interest. This was an American entry by some young architects from Philadelphia: Giovanni Cosco, Nathaniel East, Samuel Galbreath, Richard Huffman, and Russell Weeks. Their scheme covered almost all of the site but rose up less high than the winning solution. It was insistently "conventional" in approach (for example, it had modest structural spans and bay sizes), the presentation text was turgid but seemed principled, and the design was honest with unpretentious originality, except for a rather weird if likeable conceptual notion: a large copied piece of Alvar Aalto's famed (and destroyed) Viipuri Library, a 1927 competition winner in Finnish Karelia, was resurrected and transplanted within the scheme as an homage to Aalto.

After this, the anonymity of all entries was lifted by M. Regard. According to apocryphal stories later, the jury thought, on stylistic grounds, that the special mention project was the work of Robert Venturi's firm in the United States. When they learned otherwise, they assumed the team members were his acolytes, as they also came from Philadelphia. The winning entry too was from America, the jury had guessed. When the sealed envelope was opened, the name "Piano & Rogers" was read out. Silence. No one had the least idea who they were. "In consultation with Ove

Arup and Partners, Consultant Engineers." Everyone knew of the Arup firm. "Thank God we are all right," it was reputed someone said. Prouvé declared later that Johnson had been the scheme's great champion, and the two of them had together pushed it through.

In the Jury Report published several months later jointly by the Ministries of National Education and Cultural Affairs, the introduction applauded the competition's attraction to young firms and felt sure the winner was excellent and the runners-up all had great merit. It said the jury was somewhat disquieted overall, however, by a certain lack of originality that showed itself in "tortured expressionism, extravaganza, paroxysm, excess" on the one hand, or a functional grayness that fell "into real banality" on the other hand: "compact and undifferentiated volumes that could be a hospital as easily as a museum."

Further along in the Jury Report, the very liberal conditions for the competitors were defended. No constraints on expression had been imposed, nor on height or other limits; even the competition program was subject to competitors' modification, if justified, without being declared *hors de concours* in advance for that. All this showed, it said, in the multiplicity of approaches: schemes with the accommodation half buried or completely buried as craters; schemes with the accommodation lifted high on pilotis; some that assiduously greeted the neighborhood in their forms, and through all sorts of walkways; some that denied the surroundings in towers, symbolic monuments, geometrical forms, "experiments in a pure aesthetic or in monumentality." The jury felt they, too, had to be eclectic in their range of final choices, to encourage architects throughout the world who were seeking new modes of expression.

One criterion that particularly figured in the judgment was good lighting. The jury thought that a library and a museum shouldn't be deprived of natural light. An otherwise attractive scheme was rejected because it put the museum in the basement. And the jury had strong feelings about the importance of good internal and external communications; hence their appreciation of the winning scheme. Also, they commented on the fact that "50 projects relied on geometric forms":

> If the jury almost instantly—and always unanimously—rejected spheres and cubes, cones and cylinders, inverted (or uninverted) pyramids, and giant ovoid forms, even if these projects should be, on the whole, perfectly constructible, they did not want to mark by that an absolute opposition to any building conceived as a combination of geometric elements; their choice of certain finalists and even the winning project showed that well. But the jury considered that, if the freedom of architectural form should be encouraged, this freedom cannot be merely formal; that a "monument" is vain that would have no other function besides expressing an architectural "gesture," that emphasis is not necessarily eloquence, and that "art for art's sake" can be the contrary of art.

As for the jury's analysis of the winning project, this is a slightly shortened English version of the Jury Report text.

> The principal characteristics of [the winning] project are the following:
>
> • The building only occupies half of the Plateau Beaubourg. The other half is occupied by a long square, a little sunken. . . . This vast open space. . . should serve numerous lively activities. On the other hand, the space allows one enough distance for a good view of the Centre.
>
> • The building has forms that are simple, and have a great span (50m high, 150m long, 50m deep). The architects have avoided giving it a compact and massive aspect; it rests on pilotis; the surface beneath is completely separated. [The open ground floor had

to be modified later.] The simplicity and geometric regularity of the structure and the articulation of facades should also give an impression of lightness and transparency.

• The exterior aspect of the Centre should be very lively and animated. The escalators, elevators, and freight elevators to serve public circulation, transport of goods and artworks will contribute to the animation of the main facade, on which, in addition, information about activities inside and outside will be projected.

• The construction is conceived in such a way that it can evolve as a function of needs: floor decking 50m long was envisaged, and ceilings 50m x 15m without a single column. The flexibility of interior spaces is very great as a result. Aside from that, the volumes are inserted between steel tube verticals forming lattices 60m high. These too can be modified without nullifying the spirit of the project.

• The technical realization of the building should take place under favorable conditions:

—Not much excavating underground. As a result, no difficult shoring.

—A structure permitting a relatively easy placement on site.

—Safety of the fire prevention system, due to circulation of water in the tubular framework.

The text goes on to describe the allocation of the Centre's activities, some of which were reallocated in later design development (such as the contemporary events area and the industrial design center, at first placed under the Rue de Renard). It then tries to deal with the main issue: just why this scheme was chosen as winner. The report puts clearly the emphases and enthusiasms of the jurors:

This project was chosen almost unanimously (eight votes out of nine).

What are the reasons for this choice? In what way did this project respond better than any other to the underlying intentions of the program?

1. Above all, the brief expressed the desire to have at its disposal a "functional," "flexible," "polyvalent" construction—that is, adaptable as much as possible to needs, means, and tastes that are changeable and unforeseeable.

The project presented responds to all these requirements as follows:

—Simplicity of spaces: one could dream of the possible uses of several great decks 150m long and 50m wide—7500m sq. per level, without a column.

—Ease of public circulation (escalators on the facade), and of material transport (extra space underground; freight elevators on the facades).

—Exterior spaces much more extensive than envisaged (this is important for the presentation of sculpture, exhibitions, open air performances, etc.)

—Simplicity of communications inside the Centre.

—Finally, the possibility of altering exterior volumes of the Centre without nullifying the spirit of the project.

2. If the adaptation of form to function was carried out remarkably in the winning scheme, that scheme still had to conform to the mandate of the program for "an architectural and urban form that represents our era."

In what way did the winning scheme respond to this requirement, the most important one and also the most difficult one to satisfy?

—The building, first and foremost. In appearance, its form is simple. But one does not know many buildings resembling this one: not a tower or a skyscraper, but, seen from afar, an immense screen, and closer, a mirror offering a constantly changing play of images and reflections.

—In addressing oneself only to the construction, one judges only half the scheme. In fact, the winning architects did not merely conceive of a construction with hardly an equivalent in the world. They also discovered an apt and subtle equilibrium between a building of great expanse, largely open and exposed, and on the other hand, exterior spaces—squares, gardens, various walkways—at the same time separated, intimate, and protected. If they were not the only ones to propose an architectural creation of the first rank, they were incontestably the only ones to organize the space they had in such a way that, in spite of its relatively reduced dimensions, it took on an unexpected and even unhoped-for vastness—and with so much mastery in the invention, that the simplicity of the employed means made one forget the complexity of the difficulties that they were the only ones to resolve.

—Finally, if in certain epochs one found it necessary to hate "movement that displaces lives" and to look for the canons of an immobile beauty, our time loves movement, and even the boiling-over of life. In its exterior forms, the winning project has certainly been conceived with a great simplicity and a great linear purity (reinforced by the deliberate dryness of the drafting), but everything is done to draw out, to stimulate, and to keep life there: there is the placement "in the entry-way" of the most creative and animated activities, the contemporary events area, the permanent gallery of design; then, there is the constant exchange with the neighborhood made partly through pedestrian circulation, and connected to the Centre with an open-air space which should not be a gloomy esplanade, but a meeting place, a place for gathering, for entertainment, a constant focus of animation and movement; there is the captivating effect of the public circulation, visible through the glass partitions, and by the public ascent in escalators perpetually moving, a unique climbing column attracting passers-by in the square; there is the gaiety and life, finally, of a great facade treated like a screen that can reflect, in the passage of days, all the spectacles of the world.

To sum up, if the winning scheme was striking in a simplicity that contrasted with other much more complex efforts, this simplicity was not simplistic: that was apparent. It would be a gross misunderstanding to think that the jury's choice, arrived at in the first round of scrutiny, is not explained by conviction, but—despairing of reason, and chosen out of resignation—merely by a preference for a reassuring simplicity.

Knowing that it had been called to judge the results of an "ideas competition," the jury in fact considered that the project it chose—as early as the first round of scrutiny, and with near-unanimity among hundreds of other projects, all very carefully studied and occasionally excellent (as the analysis of the finalists shows)—responded perfectly, as much by its technical qualities as by its architectural worth, to the hopes raised for the great enterprise decided by the President of the Republic in December, 1969.

On July 15, 1971, this report hadn't been written yet. But the jury's enthusiasm and conviction that was later expressed in these words got communicated at once informally, lending the winners the encouragement they needed on arrival in Paris, and they somehow sustained it with their own shrewdness and tact in the next few days. The more experienced among them knew that architectural competitions were sometimes won in a day, but lost the following week, when confidence in the winners was dashed.

. . . . . .

Richard Rogers, Ruth Elias, John Young, and his girlfriend Ange Linney all flew out immediately. Su Rogers arrived with John Miller, an architect friend. Others of the London Piano & Rogers staff—the secretary Sally Appleby, and Peter Flack—drove from London and arrived in Paris the next morning. Renzo Piano, who had been sailing when he first got the message, was there already, as was Gianni Franchini from Genoa. Peter Rice hadn't at first received the telegram sent to Arup from Paris, but had heard via Rogers and, before he caught a plane himself, had located Ted Happold in Lancaster where Happold had been considering a job as professor of engineering at the university. Rice's wife was late in pregnancy and didn't come. Happold's wife wouldn't come—she had been to prize givings before. Before Happold left England, he rang old Ove Arup and told him the news. Arup said, "Oh dear! Oh dear! You know these jobs have a funny habit of ending up in the hands of the local architects!" It was made to sound a humorous observation, but it was no less than the truth. Happold noticed that the congratulations came second, very real and heartfelt though they were. The order of precedent was something that braced Happold's determination on the Beaubourg job for a long time.

To the winners, the first four or five days were incredible. On their way through customs, the passport controllers spotted most of them and raised their hands, whereupon attachés collected them. Latecomers were chauffeured directly to the reception, where cameras were waiting. The news had broken in England and Italy in a subdued way, but in France, the winning of the Beaubourg competition called for major media coverage. For years afterward the prizewinners were told by scores of Frenchmen and women that they first saw them on television being officially received and fêted—these young, almost callow-looking English and Italian men, and very attractive Englishwomen, who were all so informally dressed.

Actually, Happold had stopped in London to collect his dinner jacket, just in case it proved to be that sort of event, and also to pack what he called his "civil engineer's suit"—a dignified dull blue model. The architects never dressed up, but even if they had decided to make an effort on this occasion, the expected attire in Paris was utterly beyond their imagination. The clothes worn at the time are almost central to their memories. Preponderantly dressed in jeans, John Young, Ruth Elias, Richard Rogers, Renzo Piano, and Gianni Franchini were first taken to the Louvre for a few delighted introductions, and then almost immediately they were rushed aboard a Seine *bateau mouche*. They grasped that the glittering boat was set for a banquet in their honor with white tablecloths and abundant flowers, and was crowded with hundreds of people in long gowns and white ties. These weren't just guests, they were *dignitaries,* wearing decorations. Government and diplomatic figures were there, as well as Bordaz and the assessing jury. It seemed completely incredible that this distinguished crowd of high officials and eminent architects was waiting, with enthusiastic curiosity, to lionize award winners whom they had never met and had mostly never even heard of. Really, it was beyond a fairy tale: even Cinderella had been looked over first before being proclaimed the new Princess.

The winners were divided up among the tables. Young tried to recall his school French without a lot of success. During the splendid dinner that none of them afterward remembered a bite of, they were told that only one juror had voted against them, and their entry had been singled out in the very first round.

More disconcertingly, they were advised that their construction timetable was missing. For the competition entry, the Arup engineers had in the end followed their convictions with a conservatively thought-through timetable showing that the job had to take six years. Actually, no such exacting analysis was required for the submission, and it would have influenced the jury adversely (Richard Rogers didn't even realize that the engineers had lengthened the specified timetable). Perhaps the excision was done by a favoring juror—Philip Johnson was mentioned—or by the programmation team. No one ever found out. Happold was shocked, then amused, by this story. It seemed to bear out his worst view of winning competitions: people don't want to look that bloody close, they only see what they want to see.

The next day was set up for the presentation session. The winners were taken in the morning to the Grand Palais and into the hall, and there in the distance on a big display was their entry, much enlarged. Walking along toward the display through the vast space, Piano said to Happold, "Isn't it terrifying, Ted." "It really is," agreed Happold; "I feel we shouldn't be here." "Should we write and apologize to all these people?" Piano said. They were shown floor after floor of the Grand Palais filled with entries, all 680 others. This represented something like 2,600 man-years of work, one of the winners remembers being told. It was depressing, and showed something else about competitions—the wasted effort involved on the part of the losers. An apology suddenly didn't seem so unjustified.

The session was not quite an extension of what had begun the day before at the Louvre. It was a sort of expanded press conference with photographers, TV cameras, and some of the public, including disappointed competitors. They were in a very big auditorium full of people. One of the winners was expected to speak. Rice tried to get Happold to do it since he was about ten years older than the others, but he refused, so Piano spoke. His French was not much better than anyone else's, but as a fellow Latin he managed to get by. Then came questions, and their next big shock: this was a critical crowd expecting some kind of redress. Unlike the gathering the evening before, it appeared that no one in this packed auditorium actually seemed to like the scheme. Some people were bitter that such a design had won. One woman became so vituperative about modern design in general and the scheme in particular that she was removed by the police. Piano had a presentiment during this event. He suddenly realized that the French actually planned to build Beaubourg, and this meant the design team was now willy-nilly part of French political life.

The winners next found themselves in a little preliminary business meeting. They were sure by this time that the French had cynically expected to receive a group of mindless stylists from Paraguay (as it were), that a carve-up of the job was imminent among all the hovering French competition advisers, and that the winners were expected to tie in with them and hand over control of the design, if not the whole job. They heard that the job might actually go ahead if they were ready to accept normal French fee scales (about 6 percent of the total construction cost for the entire team), to start work immediately, and to finish the building in five years. Piano & Rogers had understood the brief to have said that fees would be 6 percent for architects alone, as in Britain. The team saw that the low fee for architects really meant the typical French practice of leaving design detail to others.

That French tie-ups were expected seemed abundantly clear. A French contractor whom Happold once had known very slightly rang him up and gave him an open invitation to lunch as soon as he was able to come. Most of the winners had been put by the government into the Sofitel Bourbon, an expensive hotel. Piano & Rogers had no money, but sooner or later the architects expected a check for their prize (actually it arrived weeks afterward), and they just hoped it would come before the hotel bill had to be paid (the bill was still being argued about two years later; the design team finally paid it, but only for their traveling companions); meanwhile they asked if Happold's friend would buy them lunch too. Happold consulted his acquaintance and found he would be more than delighted. That was all the encouragement needed: twelve hungry winners showed up, hoping the French tax authorities allowed such expenses.

Su Rogers was one of the bona fide winners, having contributed to the competition at least to the extent of insisting that the firm enter, and she had continued to manage the office of Piano & Rogers. But she understandably found the triumph a bit difficult to take. She calmly told Rogers, Ruth Elias, and Piano that the marital split would be permanent; then she and Miller went back to London. Peter Rice needed to go home because his wife was about to give birth. The next day the winners were to meet Georges Pompidou, so who would take the five places specified was the burning question. The honor most appropriately belonged to Richard Rogers, Su Rogers, Renzo Piano, Gianni Franchini, Peter Rice, and Ted Happold. As Su Rogers and Peter Rice were leaving, John Young could be added. The deserving five were ready the next morning to be received by the president of the Republic.

A Citroën from the Élysée Palace arrived at the hotel for their use. It motored to the palace and around the arc of the drive. The winners went up a great flight of stairs and into an antechamber, and to their surprise they saw the enormous display with their blown-up competition design, which no doubt had been very laboriously moved from the Grand Palais. They were shown into the reception room. There were five very low elegant chairs facing a huge desk, behind which was a large and quite high chair. At the end of the desk was a lady with grey hair, irreproachably dressed. She was the translator. Pompidou came in briskly and sat down in his thronelike chair behind the desk. His audience agreed later that they all noticed the same thing: the soles of his shoes were polished. And Pompidou began by noticing too, looking down carefully along the row in front of him. He saw an exhibit of self-presentation not consciously calculated, and certainly completely unstudied as a group effect. And yet it said something, in its artless way, which may have given a not unsatisfying impression.

At one end was Happold, the oldest, in his civil engineer's suit. He was wearing a depressing tie to match. Next to him was Renzo Piano. Piano, always rather an Anglophile, was wearing one of the tweeds of the type known as "thornproof," which isn't thought to look authentic unless it is unpressed and slightly baggy. His brown thornproof suit went well with his longish beard. Next was Rogers, wearing a suit that French railway drivers wear, of faded denim, to which he had added a flower-power-type shirt, with no tie. Next was Franchini, wearing a Miami Beach–style striped white jacket, and odd trousers. Finally, at the end of the row, John Young was there, wearing a red Mickey Mouse sweatshirt. No one is certain any longer whether the sweatshirt actually had a picture of Mickey Mouse on it, but it was unarguably in that category. Much later, in reflecting on the ensemble they presented, they were sure that Young's attire was the reason they clinched the job.

Pompidou observed them for only a moment and then began a long and inspiring peroration about how they were going to be the cause of much controversy, just as Claude Perrault had been when he designed the east front of the Louvre. And how they weren't going to work for Pompidou, the mere politician, but for Paris, the greatest and most beautiful city, which meant they worked for France, the most cultured, discerning, and enchanting country. His words were heartwarming, charming, very learned, and utterly convincing. At the end of the speech he said, Have you any questions? The winners had been joking about the prize money and whether they would ever get it in time to prevent being brought to court as vagrants. Rogers had been most seriously worried about the hotel bill, and it was he who said, "Yes, I have a question." Piano and Happold exchanged panic-stricken looks. "Excuse me, but could I possibly have your autograph?" Rogers said. "It's for my children. They'll never believe we were here."

Pompidou laughed and said, "Ask my secretary." He got up and came around the desk, shaking hands. The winners noticed how short he was. "You are the capitalist of the group," he said to Happold, and they all laughed. Then he left, and his secretary started producing signed photographs. A minute later, like the Wizard of Oz coming out from behind the array of tricks, Pompidou was back looking totally different: his jacket was off, his shoulders were slouching, a cigarette was dangling from his mouth. Speaking fair English, he talked energetically about design with the group. This lasted for more than an hour. Finally, they were so late that there was a flurry and a fuss: someone rushed in and helped Pompidou back into his jacket. The team had to be shown out. There was a guard of honor drawn up, but no car. As they wondered if they should review the guard, the official Citroën limousine again swept into the drive, with the president of Brazil inside. The winners had been so long that their car had been sent for him. After that meeting, none of them ever saw Pompidou again.

It was too late for lunch, and a meeting at about 3 P.M. was scheduled with Bordaz. The five had an unshakeable suspicion that trouble might really be in store—that Bordaz's Délégation would make the project impossible by presenting demands they were unable to comply with. So they went into a bar and wrote out a list of about 20 demands of their own: they wanted a design contract, an office immediately, a certain amount of money, and so on—defensive counterdemands. Arriving exactly on time, they found only Bordaz and Regard ahead of them. Other officials started arriving fifteen minutes later, but by then the meeting was practically over. (Much later, they learned from Bordaz that he had gone in to see Pompidou straight after the team had left.

Pompidou had told Bordaz he thought they would be all right. "They can do it, and they have style," was Happold's summary of the exchange.) At the meeting, the winners immediately showed Bordaz their list, and he pulled out a pencil and checked every point: some money, yes; office, yes, you can move into the Grand Palais for the moment; negotiated contract, yes—Bordaz agreed to everything apart from the exact fee and contract details. Whether or not the rest of the Délégation had consigned the Piano & Rogers–Arup team to the grave, by the time they finally drifted into the meeting, the winners were off and running.

Southwest corner of Beaubourg with X-pattern high tensile steel cross-bracing, the rods 60mm (2 3/8″) in diameter. In the structural design, the cross-bracing was overprovided to allow for partial redundancy, as where it has been omitted for access to the building from the escalators at the top level

4 Setting up in Paris

There were several more tough, exploratory meetings with the Délégation in the first days while the winners were still treated as if they were very important. A few of the team who gaily rode on the back of an open car were stopped by police. They were amazed that nearby cars stopped too, and French government men fanned out of them flashing credentials, making clear that this crew were not to be arrested. Public recognition at the time was scant, but the team's brief pink period went on while heavy pressures started to be applied.

Despite Bordaz's initial support, the contract and fee were still unsettled. Forty-eight hours after meeting Pompidou, the design team was back with Bordaz, fighting for the power to control the project. They were offered a four-month contract for about £5,000, which was obviously intended to give the client the option of getting rid of winners who were proving undesirable at a minimum cost. P & R's answer was to fly in George Stringer, then the Royal Institute of British Architects' consultant solicitor, to help negotiate a reasonable contract.

After a difficult day's negotiation Stringer and the team succeeded in raising their fees to about £50,000 over six months, though they did not manage to fix up an ongoing contract. The team canceled their flights home that had been booked in the expectation of negotiation failure. At the end of the six-month contract the team were expected to complete an *avant projet sommaire* (APS), a stage of work that in normal French architectural practice included a preliminary design, a construction program, and a cost plan.

Plenty still remained unsettled, as they were well aware. The French officials they had negotiated with could not see why the winners were demanding high fees, using as an excuse British-style design control. The design team could not see why the French should want to change the successful means of working that the Anglo-Italian winners were used to. Moreover, the winners suspected that the programmation group was antipathetic to their scheme; they had heard a rumor that their favorite was the runner-up. Whatever the truth of that, Lombard and his colleagues had certainly been instructed to bear down hard. They insisted that the building really did have to be finished in five years.

If this was to be attempted, the design aspect the engineers felt least secure about was the lifting system to vary the height of the floors. Rice said to Rogers, "In the time scale they're demanding we'll never solve that." Happold gloomily agreed. Rogers assured them that though he liked the idea he had never believed in it; he had never reckoned it was technically feasible anyway. Stacking up the odds against timely completion still further, a new element was being added to the program: IRCAM, an experimental musical and acoustical research center, the directorship of which would be offered to Pierre Boulez to lure him back from America. And apart from relegating the responsibility for this also to the design team in their APS, so far no one had said anything about overall building costs.

The winners briefly returned home to London and Genoa with the first steps taken toward getting their scheme built, but they were not very optimistic. With the short-term contract condition, no one felt like moving permanently to France. Piano and Rogers thought that Happold should live there for a while. Happold had many other responsibilities at Arup, and couldn't. This was also true of Rice. Rogers maintained that he didn't know how even to go about buying a pencil in Paris. It was a way of saying what they all knew: difficulties of working in France that they couldn't even imagine awaited them. Finally a scratched-together team was formed to work on the APS contract, a few members of which were contributing for the first time. Piano, Rogers, Benedetto Merello (from the Genoa office), Young, and Happold commuted from home. Marco Goldschmied moved to Paris for most of the period, and Franchini lived there through all of that period without money. The architects slept together in hotel double beds.

While the APS was in process, Su Rogers decided to wind up her participation in the office. Her background as a sociologist and urban planner wasn't critical at the design development stage, so she wasn't indispensable in Paris. Besides, she had the three young Rogers children to see to in London, plus John Miller, with whom she was living, and his two children (Miller and she later married). She made a final break with Piano & Rogers, and the others agreed to buy out her share of the partnership. There was a lot of money at stake in Beaubourg's fees, or at least the principals hoped so.

Despite smooth progress for the moment, the Arup part of the team had been worrying about their own involvement. Their role was important and included some design that enriched the architects' own responsibilities—the planning of the traffic and pedestrian circulation systems, for example. Though they had shared the competition triumph with Piano & Rogers, they feared that the client was making simplistic distinctions between the architect's "creative" and the engineer's "technical" roles, to their eventual disadvantage (despite contrary, but equally plausible, evidence that the Arup practice was well appreciated for its substance and reputation). They were concerned about the possibility of being replaced with French engineers. This was no idle fear, especially if the client didn't perceive the engineering of Beaubourg as a creative task and only expected professional technical administration. They were anxious about a shotgun wedding between the design team and a separate *Bureau d'Études Techniques,* in accordance with the usual French working method. Lombard especially thought Arup's work to be too slow and unnecessarily exacting at that stage; too "English." But in December 1971 the six-month APS contract stage was completed with a new model, a report, a construction analysis, and a modified timetable, all to the satisfaction of the client, which allayed a few fears.

The APS was presented by Tony Dugdale, Benedetto Merello, and Gianni Franchini, later assisted by Alan Stanton, Mike Davies, and Chris Dawson, all overseen by John Young. Though it won interim approval, enthusiasm for it came mainly from Pompidou, Bordaz, and the administrators—it didn't do as well with the professionals. Sandberg of the Stedelijk came and said they had lost direction. P & R and Arup knew the APS was perhaps further from a final design than the original scheme had been, and they themselves weren't very satisfied.

The work was meticulous, but the APS submission had drifted away from the competition design in some crucial respects. The original scheme was praiseworthy for boldness, grand simplicity, and flexibility. Even the competition model showed it—the submitted photos were a montage of a few re-used pieces. The APS design was a little like a celebrated young author's misjudged second novel: its scope had been unsafely expanded, and perhaps it took a little too much for granted. In an attempt to be more practical about the use of steel, the building's extremely long and thick main girders had been turned into Vierendeel trusses (trusses with rectangular openings in the web), and to help justify their new five-meter depth, the openings encompassed service floors between the public floors. But the attempt at economy didn't work. The trusses needed so much added material in the rectangular corners that the design was using three times as much steel as expected (and three times as much as they finally used; the discovery of a much more thrifty solution was several months in the future). Partly to offset the Vierendeel design's steel costs, the competition design's simple rectangular steel cage with occasional voids—a latticework against the sky—had given way to a solid wedding-cake structure, its open decks mostly mere rooftops amid the tiered setbacks. The APS redesign had an unconvincing (and worse, unconvinced) quality. Its edges and extensions had become transparent capsules or lozenges. The rounded corners, so very mid-1960s, were familiar to magazine readers of the day as shapes much favored in conceptual proposals by the English Archigram group. Because of them the second model was unkindly dubbed "the jelly-mold scheme" by a few members of the team.

The APS was formally approved in March 1972. Pompidou's personal liking for it didn't hurt. "He liked it because he could describe it with his hands," said Rogers. Cascading lower ends north and south gave the impression it would fit in with its neighbors better. So the new soft form, high in the center and low at the ends, also became known as "the Pompidou section."

But however dissatisfied the design team was, the interim APS scheme did achieve its main task of building the client's confidence in their skills. As soon as it became likely that a new contract would be on offer, the Arup practice decided they would have to open an office in Paris (though a few more months passed before they did). Michael Barclay, one of the Structures 3 lieutenants who had already been working on Beaubourg, spoke good French and was keen to lead the office. The architects were ready to make their presence more permanent too.

To hire architectural staff, Piano & Rogers never put any ads in the papers. Most assistants either came from architectural schools Piano or Rogers had taught at, or applicants wrote in for jobs. Two or three just-graduated French students were recommended, and joined them. Two Australians heard about the project and were recruited. Before the APS, Rogers had brought in a few people he had known at the London Architectural Association School of Architecture, including Tony Dugdale, who was teaching at Cornell; Dugdale talked to Alan Stanton, who had worked for Norman Foster but was then in California with Mike Davies and Chris Dawson. They all came, their average age under 30.

Laurie Abbott, who had worked for Rogers before, was much appreciated despite his surly appearance and manner. Abbott had unsuccessfully applied for about 30 jobs before Rogers finally looked at his portfolio and hired him. He was a brilliant draftsman-technician. At that time many architects still used messy India ink nibs that got clogged, especially those for producing the finer lines. Abbott took the unheard-of trouble of filing down his 00 nibs in order to draw lines that were like gossamer. Rogers was sure that Beaubourg would need someone with Abbott's capacity for taking pains.

At the job interview of Eric Holt, who later became leader of the group doing development of the facades, Holt said, "I want to be involved with this building. I think it will be the most important building of the century. I want to be able to look back in the years ahead and say I helped do it." Most of the growing team were motivated that way.

The administrative setup in the design team's office was settled slowly. Piano and Rogers had new people to work with, and *faute de mieux* they were obliged to be open and experimental about responsibilities in order to see what they could really do. Stanton, Davies, and Dawson had formed a group called Chrysalis that did lightweight structures, and they arrived from California expecting an opportunity to do much the same on Beaubourg's piazza. They had presumed that the original competition team was developing the building design, but after a short while, they realized that most of the design need was for the building itself. Only about ten architects were yet there, plus a few students. The work just had to be done, and lightweight structures were obviously well down the list of priorities.

The building's flexible framework was also proving a conceptual framework. Subject to continual change, everything needed attention, so people began to cut the action out for themselves and define what they were doing. Some fell by the wayside without a role. John Young and Marco Goldschmied returned to England in the spring of 1972, since there was some P & R work there and neither was willing to stay in Paris permanently. Sometimes there were battles between individuals or teams when Piano and Rogers were busy elsewhere. As a result, the group leaders who emerged knew something about what they were doing, or at least were able to impress others that way. At several times Piano and Rogers decided to employ a "coordinator" for Paris so they themselves could duck administration and concentrate on Beaubourg's design, as well as other work in their London and Genoa offices. The most notable recruits for the job were Bill Carmen, an experienced U.S. architect, and Martin Richardson, a British architect. The rest of the team were already moving twice as fast as the coordinators could, and neither was able to catch up or last for long. The idea of hiring someone to represent the team to the client was also tried, but it never worked. Human costs rose as careers were advanced or sidetracked.

Richard Rogers and Renzo Piano worked together well. (Since they hadn't done a finished building together before Beaubourg, and afterward decided only to act as consultants for each other's work, Beaubourg—with IRCAM—was their only joint effort. Of course it was enough; bigger than most architects' lifetime work.) Marriages of people very much alike and those of people very different can both be successful. Piano and Rogers were a bit of each: alike in general outlook, different in particular interests and temperament. Rogers concerned himself with everything, and he would hound people aggressively or try to inspire them enthusiastically. According to Su Rogers, he had a genuine reverence for democratic teamwork but really tended to decide things himself. Piano loved the opportunities Beaubourg gave him to research architectural improvement by industrial methods. He had always enjoyed working on precise problems concerning the logic of things and was taking that kind of interest in the structure; his method of leadership was tactful and avuncular. Peter Rice, the engineer most centrally involved in Beaubourg's creative achievements (especially after the third year) was diplomatic, articulate, an able strategist, "best of all, optimistic," as Rogers said; this was profoundly necessary in a building where so much was at the very edge of possibility. Lennart Grut, involved with structures, and Tom Barker, with mechanical equipment, filled out the complement of key engineers. According to Piano the team members "had disagreements very often, but there were no real problems."

In the subjective view of some of the architects, the Beaubourg architects became more easily acclimated to Paris than the engineers. The architects were younger and tended to be more easygoing. The engineers weren't as unconventional (especially the mechanical equipment engineers); they were more likely to have spouses and children. New members of the design team had to find places to live and to start moving their families. The hard work and foreign location didn't inevitably produce marital difficulties, but there were some problems in that respect. Many families had to move to the Paris suburbs, and spouses were stuck out there with small children. With a foreign wife's husband at work in town from 8:30 A.M. to 8:30 P.M. and no opportunity to cadge the sort of neighborly baby-sitting in St. Germain that might be promoted amid one's own clan in New Ash Green near London, there were strains. Another problem dogged a few of the engineers, many of whom at first were flying to Paris Monday morning and flying home Friday afternoon: some got lonesome. In the course of events, only one design team member got involved with the wife of another—though that section took a temporary nosedive while the Romeo was being fired (they fired the more talented guy, a colleague said afterward).

Piano and Franchini spoke the best French and fared best with Frenchmen. To the French, an Italian accent was like a French accent to the English: slightly romantic and advantageous. ("The French look on the English as rivals, but they view themselves as more rational Italians," said Rice, who believed it was crucial for Piano to have been on the team in order for the French to have agreed to build with them.) Others of the team were sure that their overall incapacity in French was an advantage. They were thereby shielded from critical mutterings, though blatant objections would reach them well enough. In the building industry, it is not unusual to find speakers of different languages working together effectively. A few considered that their language problems had the advantage of making the building the main means of communication, since people who could barely speak to each other would have to talk and draw at the same time. But those who believed this got their comeuppance when French colleagues appeared on the scene—

neither colleague, contractor, nor client would bother with a complete non-Francophone.

After the APS approval, Piano and Rogers both started to spend more time in Paris. Rogers, Dugdale, Merello, and Franchini shared one room for months, with short breaks. In June 1972 Ruth Elias left her London job and moved with Rogers to a small apartment in the Marais in Paris. She sometimes helped the office to write reports and did graphic design work (she had been an art director at Penguin Books), but her main activity was looking for a better place for them both to live. Piano too was searching for stylish living quarters. After some years, he found a large apartment in the Rue Ste. Croix de la Bretonnerie, and when Beaubourg was complete, it became his joint-venture office with Rice. About 18 months before Beaubourg's completion, Ruth Elias, or Mrs. Rogers as she then was, finally found magnificent accommodation for them in the Place des Vosges. Fixing up the large duplex apartment was a project that rivaled Beaubourg, she later contended.

French banks were unwilling to grant P & R the business loans necessary to run the job and cover their overheads between payments. On dozens of occasions Rogers had to be in London arguing about overdrafts with the National Westminster Bank, insisting that Beaubourg would be worth it. Rising income and useful fringe benefits finally meant that the cash situation was better for a while. Rogers would try to talk over these things with Piano at lunch, which they almost always had together, but Piano generally refused to discuss business over food. Ruth Rogers (later to become a celebrated *restauratrice*) usually cooked it. Part of her morning was typically spent in the office, then she would go to the market about an hour before lunch, rush home to cook it, then she would sit over the meal until late afternoon when Rogers would leave again with Piano for the office where both would stay until about 8:30. Every Saturday night in the Latin Quarter there was a street fight, usually broken up by the police with CS gas, they remembered—1968 wasn't that far in the past.

During the setting-up period, some vital conceptual research was done by the team's engineers into the means of using steel. Shortly after the competition victory there had been a cable roof structure conference in Tokyo, where Peter Rice had gone to deliver a paper on the design of the Arup roof in Mecca. He was shown some buildings from Expo 70 in Osaka that had remained undemolished. One of these, Kenzo Tange's theme building, included a huge cagelike space frame. The frame joints, or nodes, were as big as basketballs. It reminded Rice of the German MERO system of tubular strut members for light roofs, but on a vast scale. Tange's steel structure was a great eye-opener for him, especially because it was made of cast steel, like the Munich structure that had impressed Happold.

In the nineteenth century, iron construction had taken on immediate prestige with the building of the 1851 London Crystal Palace. The New York Crystal Palace was soon built of similar materials, as were many other structures for which glass and steel seemed appropriate such as exhibition halls and the train sheds of railway terminals; later, skylights, theater roofs, and rows of iron-framed industrial buildings were constructed. Since iron doesn't burst into flames, it was at first believed that these structures were fireproof. The truth began to emerge in 1858 when the combustible contents of the New York Crystal Palace caught fire and the structure collapsed within fifteen minutes: iron drastically changes in high temperature. It has a dramatic loss of strength at above 550° centigrade. Indeed, iron buildings on fire are more dangerous to people inside than heavy timber buildings, which burn but don't tend to collapse suddenly. After a few more iron buildings caught fire and collapsed spectacularly, the principle of

loss of strength in heat became properly understood, and ferrous
construction began to be used on public buildings in most parts of
the world only under conditions where the metal could be
protected against any rapid rise in temperature to the collapse
point, almost always by encasing it in an insulating material such
as concrete, expanded mineral fiber, or special plaster.

The structural capabilities of the metal had also become much
better understood since the early days. In iron's early use, it was
simply melted and cast. Later it was wrought—pounded with
hammers when hot—to improve its elasticity and tensile
strength—its muscular resistance to bending and pulling. Still
later the iron was alloyed with carbon to make steel, which was
stronger yet. Steel was drawn through rollers while red hot. This
changed its crystalline structure as it cooled, and made the steel
better in tension than wrought iron. Thus, for architectural
construction the ferrous technology of mere casting had been long
left behind. It had almost been forgotten, until the structures of
Munich and Osaka appeared. The casting process was associated
with a microstructure of large iron crystals that had made the
material very unsatisfactory in tension. Was this on the way to
being overcome? If so, wasn't fire safety still a daunting constraint?

In Osaka, Rice talked to Koji Kamiya, the job architect of the
theme building, and Kawaguchi, the engineer who had designed it
with Tange. Ferrous castings stood up relatively well against fire
and corrosion, and as modern castings could meet specific structural
requirements too, Rice went home with the perception (as Happold
had also heard) that the combination of centrifugally spun cast
tubes plus cast nodes had worked out very favorably. Obviously the
traditional wisdom about castings was mostly prejudice, Rice
thought. At Beaubourg, the feasibility of having tensile cast tubes
and partly tensile nodes would only be a question of defining
carefully what they wanted to do, then checking the material

properties of different kinds of castings. At the contracting stage, a little research in the industry should find the best manufacturers to do the job. Frei Otto's 1972 Olympics stadium for Munich had cast steel joints that were being made by a firm called Pohlig. (Eventually that information led to Beaubourg's contract with Krupp, which was doing the whole Munich stadium, and a subcontract with Pohlig.)

In order to have a settled starting point at Beaubourg, fundamental decisions had to be made about basic elements. The confirmation of the radical use of cast steel, and the ways the steel would be fabricated, was the greatest of these. Rice found that everyone was supportive. As it was to define the form of the building, steel would be the only nonvarying part of the structure; the only irreplaceable element. Everything else would clip in, clip out, change over time. The steel would also define the ways change would take place because it would limit those ways. Once made, it could be attached to only in certain fashions (for example, after it received its strengthening treatment of controlled cooling, one couldn't weld to it). In confirming the use of steel, the team members were choosing a specific framework, which helpfully limited their options.

Meanwhile, much to everyone's surprise (considering that Rogers hadn't known how to buy a pencil in France), P & R and Arup had decisively chosen not to associate themselves with French professional firms, and they were going to take complete charge themselves. Part of the reason was that France had a design and construction system that was strange by British lights—or, for that matter, Italian or American ones.

Typically, French architects were expected to provide a design that was developed only in broad function and form, without detail, and without specific methods of construction. The design would then be passed over to a *Bureau d'Études Techniques*. The BET was generally a huge departmentalized office where impersonal technicians dissected and detailed the scheme expertly—though with little reference to any fundamental design intentions, or to any design concepts demanding consistency from the largest considerations to the smallest. After the BET finished its work, the general contractor was next to have a go at the project. If in the contractor's view there could be savings or more efficient construction, the client would allow further changes, again without reference to the architect's original design. To exaggerate only slightly, it was not inconceivable that a French roof could be envisaged in glass, detailed in copper, and executed in asphalt shingles.

This typical organization of the French building industry was of enormous concern to the Beaubourg architects and engineers because it took responsibility for building out of their hands. They had won the competition, and they wanted the authority and control to carry out their intentions. ("Though maybe it's not so bad," one homesick member of the design team ironically said. "At least we can get home early.")

Since French architects usually did little, they were paid little. Clients who were comfortable with the system argued that the trouble with overall design responsibility was what it would cost them. Architects in France were paid a fee equal to only about half that of professional colleagues in other countries, while the general level of salaries in France was then perhaps double that of Britain. So one way of looking at the difference between the two systems was one of professional man-hours. As a paper by Arup chiefs in an engineering journal later put it, "A French architect, engineer or *métreur* [measurer or specification writer] has about a quarter of the technical time that his British counterpart would have available, so he makes sure he has much less to do."[1]

---

1 From "Working in France" by Michael Barclay, Edmund Happold, John Martin, and Brian Watt

French architects saved costs by leaving most decisions to the BET and the contractor. This was also prudent, since French contractors had some legal liability for design as well as construction, and they bore the brunt of lawsuits. Of course the system as a whole had a number of technical and work-sharing advantages; for one thing, the great responsibilities placed on French contractors meant they had to be good ("because of the bad system," cynics said). Their doors fit. They were able to keep rain out. And contingent costs were certainly easier to absorb in their vast construction budgets. When French architects were exceptionally prepared to assume *pilotage* on a job, and to act as general contractors and site supervisors in addition to designing, they needed major financial and staff support and required much bigger fees. The Beaubourg client had neither expected nor budgeted for this.

The historic foundation of the French building system was the academic training of architects at the Paris École des Beaux-Arts, the world's oldest professional school of architecture. As happens sometimes to pioneers, the École had frozen in its tracks: its architect graduates were expected to design beautiful forms, *tout court*; they were taught that construction was not the sort of problem artists should be dealing with. As time went on, the impoverishing effects of the École des Beaux-Arts's refining discipline grew more and more marked, especially when ornamental styles gave way to modernism. The effect of this is still plainly to be seen in modern buildings throughout France, which often look oddly like full-size architectural models, as if they were cardboard made practical. (Given the procedure of their design, this is hardly more than the truth.)

---

in *The Structural Engineer,* January 1974. The article is a thorough analysis of the subject from the standpoint of British professional engineers. All the authors worked at Arup, and except for Martin, the experience of each was gained on Beaubourg.

By the early 1970s this disjointed French scheme of professional practice was being reconsidered under pressure of the more balanced polytechnic training of architects, the foreign competition, and the realization that the system wasn't as effective as it perhaps could be. The government ministries were contemplating the use of a new form of contract for architects on public buildings, but so far this hadn't affected the case of Beaubourg.

The Beaubourg team suspected that the art of architecture was actually the main victim of the BET system, especially in the more technical modern buildings. Whatever its benefits, a system that worked by divorcing concept from realization had major aesthetic disadvantages, and the most dire results were usually visited on the best designs; paradoxically, the system had fewer bad effects on routine ones. It was the most creative architects who generally found themselves defending their innovative proposals against piecemeal suggestions and changes. With design and construction carried out by a progression of specialists who supplanted each other in authority, the architect actually wound up without control. Far from being the building's *auteur* (as the *Cahiers du Cinema* might have put it), the architect in France was the person who went home early.

So having been offered the standard French deal of 6 percent for all design services after the first six-month APS contract, P & R and Arup refused it. The Établissement Public then decided to test on them the new scheme of professional contract. The essence of this reform was that public authorities would pay their professionals a commission based on a percentage of the estimate prepared by them as the realistic cost of the work, and not, as previously, based upon a percentage of the final contract sum. In part, this meant that fees could not be claimed for additional work. The substitute deal went even further to impose financial penalties against the professional designers in the event of a cost running in excess of their own estimate. If P & R and Arup agreed to the new contract, they would become a test case for the application of these new rules.

With the constraints of the new contract in mind, an estimated cost of the Beaubourg work (not erring on the side of cheapness, of course) was duly produced by Arup in late 1971—and then examined in detail by specialists appointed by the client team. At this point another lesson was learned. It was suddenly evident that the client team was becoming highly specialized too, with professional scrutineers for all the various disciplines demanded by the building: structural engineers, mechanical equipment specialists, and, for the finance and contract matters, legal officers, comptrollers, and accountants. The design team was going to have to face these other specialists regularly. There were now, for instance, staff seconded from the *Ministre de l'Economie de France,* who obviously well understood the French systems of letting and handling building contracts.

The proposed contract deal meant that if the design team was less than 12 percent off target they would earn an architect-engineer-quantity surveyor fee of 8.78 percent, if they were between 12 percent and 25 percent off they would get 7.31 percent, if they were 50 percent off they would get 4.59 percent, and so forth. This was risky, but on the other hand the design team would thereby get the professional control that it wanted, which the team members were used to in their own countries, and which indeed they desperately needed to carry out the design of Beaubourg as envisaged. With Bordaz's talent for clearing away obstacles (a talent that the team members were to admire more and more) and whispered encouragement by Jean Prouvé, P & R and Arup felt capable of taking on Beaubourg entirely without the help of French design practices.

At last a draft of the new contract was produced by the client, but back in London the Arup practice had misgivings. Povl Ahm, senior partner responsible for Happold's group, flew to Paris to talk to Happold, who had negotiated the contract. Ahm was deeply concerned, partly because he saw that Beaubourg was a way into Europe for the firm. Ahm made it clear they were depending on Happold; Happold replied that the contract wasn't what he wanted, but it was the best he could get. Ahm and Happold took the draft back to London where they had two partners' meetings over it. One senior partner in particular felt that the firm should not be made to pay any penalty to work abroad as a consultant. The Sydney Opera House had been a warning: the Utzon breakup was like the May 1968 events for the institution of Ove Arup and Partners.[2] The pressure of work at the time was very intense. After long negotiations and delays Bordaz suddenly said, in effect, Sign tomorrow, or else. Brian Watt, an Arup engineer who had been brought in as administrator on Beaubourg in the spring of 1972, was instrumental in refusing. At 3 A.M. that night in a hotel, Rogers and Piano told Happold they were going to sign the next day. In his pajamas, Happold had a last try at stopping them.

Arup's primary reason for not signing was that it hoped to remove the penalty clauses, and it believed that to stall a bit longer wouldn't matter. Not signing wasn't tantamount to giving up the job; Arup would remain professionally responsible in any case. At the final moment, P & R, while disapproving of the Arup decision, was sympathetic—the penalties could have been enormous, and if push came to shove, Arup, by keeping clear of bankruptcy through not signing, could still help P & R and save the job.

---

2 The building of the Sydney Opera House generated a major crisis in modern architectural history, as well as in Arup history. Ove Arup and Partners were engaged to provide engineering services for the Danish architect Jorn Utzon after he won the competition, and they stayed to the end even after Utzon had resigned the commission due to escalating costs and client interference. The scandal that broke over the project's vast and escalating costs owed mainly to the government client's

But not signing was a major mistake for Arup, though that only became apparent when all other problems were solved and the Arup practice was stuck with no contract. In the short run, it merely antagonized the client. Though Arup's stated reason for refusal was to be ready to back up the architects against professional liability claims, the irony was that, as far as the client was concerned, it seemed it was the architects who were willing to take on extra responsibility, for which they would be given extra reward in the form of recognized authority. The French operated strictly in accordance with official procedure, and after that, everything was channeled through the architects—every letter, order, inquiry, and meeting had to be signed for or attended by them, and the client was often to play on this. (Years later, even Arup's claims for unpaid fees had to be processed through the architects.) Small as their firm was, Piano and Rogers all at once measured up, and from a position of no capital, little credibility, and little responsibility, the architects suddenly had the lot. Though the penalties attached to extra costs or delays had seemed to Arup unfair, and as a substantial firm it had the most to lose, it ironically turned out that P & R grew powerful with the client as a result of Arup's decision.

Another decision with mixed results was the choice of quantity surveyors. Quantity surveyors have a large role in British building, though they are not much used elsewhere. Their work is to do accounting for the whole construction job: budgeting, estimating, cost-controlling prior to contract, then calculating interim expenditure during the construction program, and ultimately preparing a final account that is unlikely to be disputed because of the QS's intimate knowledge of all the goings on. Piano & Rogers ideally preferred quantity surveyors who would be independent of

---

unwillingness to own up to the true cost at any stage until near the end, for fear the high cost would have seemed irresponsible to the electorate; but when the scandal erupted, the press blamed the professionals. Though Arup felt they were innocent, they never wanted to be manipulated like that again.

P & R, Arup, and the client. But since Arup had QSes and had expected to provide them, Piano & Rogers agreed to use them (all parties later conceded that an outside QS would have been better).

Denis Stone was the chief. The QS's first task was to appraise and quickly analyze French methods and French construction contracts. The Arup team's professional experience helped, but they thought they should attach to themselves a more experienced English-speaking French national who would be able to sympathize with the cost control team's attitude, while enabling the client to communicate with them easily. The French *métreur* normally specializes in certain elements of construction or account work only. The search was difficult, and when Stone eventually found several young administrative engineers sympathetic to their needs, they were only moderately well suited to the British conception of the task.

The design team hoped that the quantity surveyor's estimate of the APS scheme would form the basis of agreed cost with the client to within a 20 percent margin. On the next phase, the *avant projet detaillé* (APD), the figure would be honed down to about 12 percent through research and further design, and this result would provide the agreed target as far as the new professional contract was concerned. The thoroughness of the QS work on the APS estimate seemed to create a good impression with the client, but it was an imperfect sort of appreciation. It took three attempts to settle costings on the APS phase (and 20 months more for the APD, while the client was demanding it in six).

Another administrative innovation was that Arup proposed using a management contractor for the whole job. This concept didn't exist in France either, though in certain respects it resembled the French *pilotage.* Management contractors were sometimes employed outside France on jobs where size, complexity, uncertainties, or—

especially—the technically creative participation of builders was at issue. (In the past 20 years, they have become much more usual in the construction industry worldwide.) Hired by the client, they work for a fee, which is generally a percentage of the building cost. To keep clear of conflicting interests, they don't do any building work themselves, but they advise the design team and assist in dividing up the work into separate contract packages. On a job where time is a crucial issue, they help by saving contract time, and on a job where costs are crucial, they help by keeping prices from escalating. After numerous interviews, the builders Grands Travaux de Marseille were chosen in the spring of 1972. The GTM management contractor was part of the package agreed with the new fee structure, and its provision was seen by the design team as the best way of getting the client, the construction industry, and, overall, the French, to accept job control by P & R and Arup.

GTM was expected to perform a number of formal functions and one informal function. The formal functions were having day-to-day site control, tendering and letting of all contracts using documents supplied by the design team, programming the logic and time-scale of how the work would be carried out (in particular, considering the phasing and interrelationships between different operating contractors), and monitoring the program. Its work was to include responsibility for quality control on site, which under other circumstances might have been undertaken by the design team.

In its informal role, GTM would act to advise the design team on the intricacies of method and operation of the French building industry. It was also expected that GTM would be more exposed than the design team to the pressures and demands that the French contractors would apply, such as the possible disapproval of radical methods and their calls for more familiar approaches. This buffering was seen as a good thing: being somewhat insulated, the design team might be able to take a slightly more elevated view of what was for everybody else an ordinary commercial proposition. By separating the design team from some industrial pressures, it was hoped that the management contractor would enable the design team to elicit advanced results that a more involved group would find difficult.

By special permission, Piano & Rogers was enrolled into the French *Ordre des Architectes*. This involved an interview at a big round table followed by a sworn oath of fealty to the principles of architecture. Professional liability insurance only applied in France to professional architects in the Ordre. The premium for the policy seemed almost equal to the coverage, but P & R thought it had no choice. (About four years later the architects realized that liability insurance was partly covered by the client, and they discovered another company willing to insure them for a twentieth of the price. They went to court to break the first policy, lost the case, and spent an extra £100,000 overall on insurance premiums as a result.) Arup was fully insured.

On the other side of the administrative table from the architects, engineers, quantity surveyors, and management contractors, the client, the Établissement Public, was more than ready to sit down. By then the client had a large, diverse organization devoted solely to establishing a functioning Centre. Its organization consisted of a number of separate groups. There were an administration staff of civil servants, the programmation group that had settled the program and continued to develop and monitor it, a construction group, and the users (the museum representatives, the library representatives, and so on).

The client administration group was principally involved with fee paying, insurance matters, and contract control. Programmation harnessed the users and produced books of documents that made up the designers' brief. Its task was to be suggestive and evaluative rather than prescriptive, leaving specific choices to the design team. The cooperation between programmation and the users it was supposed to represent wasn't entirely ideal: the museum got placed on three floors in the finished building partly because the museum representatives didn't attend meetings for a year. Pompidou later replaced the antipathetic museum head, who was under pressure from artwork donors not to move from where the art was located. Every time any user's objective changed, then spaces, equipment, and personnel probably also changed, and programmation had to keep track and keep the design team informed. It also had to withstand political and personal pressures to stick extras in. It was anticipated that the flexible Piano & Rogers design wouldn't make change orders from programmation all that difficult because it was "a very capable structure," as Lombard came to agree. But thousands of pages in many loose-leaf folders under every job heading kept Gianni Franchini fully occupied just absorbing them and making sure the right design team members heard about them.

The construction group, under André Darlot (Robert Regard had departed), was to have the most frequent direct contact with design team members. It was to receive and criticize their drawings and specifications, and to monitor design progress— initially on a week-to-week basis, but later if necessary on a day-to-day basis. It would explain construction decisions to other members of the client organization.

So the overall team that was to design and build Beaubourg had four basic elements on the organization chart:

• The design team; that is, Piano & Rogers, Architects, and Ove Arup and Partners, Engineers.

• The client, the Établissement Public du Centre Beaubourg (created by government decree), and its specialist consultants.

• The management contractor, Grands Travaux de Marseille.

• The individual contractors to be responsible for the separate subcontracts, yet to be selected.

The fact that no budget figure had at first been mentioned by the client struck the design team as either ominous or liberating, depending on their state of mind from day to day. Meanwhile, the Arup quantity surveyors were working with what they had: a design that, however much it was changing in detail, consisted of a building of a certain volume, some relatively fixed and discernible substructure costs, a superstructure that they could measure in weight of steel, and the costs of mechanical equipment and other known and approximable things required by highly serviced buildings. On the basis of what they knew, the quantity surveyors at first thought they were fulfilling their task of guiding P & R and the client on costs to within 20 percent of construction accuracy, which was an acceptable margin of error for the state of progress by the winter of 1971–72. Then at a meeting during the days of receiving acceptance for the APS scheme, one of the Établissement Public people abruptly said, "Gentlemen, you are sixty percent over." "Sixty percent over what?" the architects inquired. The client's man said, "Here is a paper showing the Ministers of Culture and Finance's joint statement about the money to be allocated to this project." The architects, severely rattled, wanted to know why they were suddenly being given this now. The client's man replied, "Because we thought if we had given it to you earlier, it would have hindered your creativity."

The APS submission seemed to blow up in the design team's faces like an exploding cigar. They were back into crisis again. The lesson Arup had learned with the Sydney Opera House was never to let costs be misrepresented. Moreover, the Arup quantity surveyors suspected that the Établissement Public's budget allocation was established on simple square-meter or cubic-meter averages for comparable types of building, not on any analysis of this particular building. The typical area or volume costs for putting up an ordinary library or art gallery could never cover Beaubourg, as their own laboriously derived costings of the actual state of the design showed. Obviously, the client had a perfect right to state a maximum sum. But what seemed most unreasonable was that the client had first chosen the design, had then insisted on the aggressive timetable, and with these fixed, was now specifying the cost. With all three parameters determined it seemed impossible, unless without losing a moment the design could somehow be refined, simplified, and economized enough so that a prospective national monument would cost no more than an ordinary institutional building. In the circumstances, all that the quantity surveyors could do was to try to point the way for the designers. First on the list because it was the most obdurate expense, yet potentially capable of the most dramatic savings, was the main steel structure.

The remaining matter that had to be resolved in setting up the job was the knotty question of the professional fee split between Piano & Rogers and Arup. Since the design team's contract had been settled solely between P & R and the client thanks to Arup's fears about the penalty clause, Arup's position was as consultant to P & R, and they had to deal with P & R over payments for their services. This took a lot of argument, brought out the worst in everybody, and wasn't settled finally for over a year. The arguments were really about making a proper analogy with matters as they might have been under British contract conditions. These were elusive for a number of reasons, such as the different extent of QS responsibilities, the value of Arup's design research, and so on. The contract solely with P & R was a background irritation that stung Arup. On their side, P & R was arguing that the professional services called for weren't the same as in Britain: QS work was mainly for the benefit of the design team, consultants had to be paid from the funds of the overall fee yet there was no idea so far who would be needed, and the fee itself would be 10.3 percent at best versus 14 or 16 percent for corresponding professional responsibilities in Britain. While these altercations went on, so did the work, but not very smoothly—especially at partner level, where job satisfaction and job performance were often severely hampered by suspicions and fears. At one point Arup offered to resign, mainly so P & R would realize it couldn't do without the engineers.

The normal fees in Britain, expressed as percentages of construction costs, might have been $5^1/_2$ percent to architects, $2^1/_2$ percent to quantity surveyors, 2 percent to structural engineers, $1^1/_2$ percent to mechanical engineers, and $2^1/_2$ percent for other consultants in lighting, acoustics, scenographics (display design), landscaping, and graphics; all making at least 14 percent total. The split of the 10.3 percent maximum fee was finally agreed to be 48 percent to P & R, 52 percent to Arup, with the former paying for acoustics, lighting, landscaping, and scenography consultancies out of their fee, the latter supplying quantity surveying within theirs.

The long uncertainty about the fee split wasn't helping to control the relative cost of professional dispensations. P & R had job security but Arup didn't, yet Arup knew it was obliged to supply its very skilled practitioners, such as materials experts, research engineers, and specialized teams. These were linked up—indeed, flown in—whenever and wherever required. P & R was more frugal. The hiring of staff and buying of office equipment were only undertaken when it had the money, which was seldom readily available. Its organization and resources were lighter, partly because it was borrowing to the hilt. For Arup, the traveling expenses, the ticking taxi meter that measured waiting time or time spent refreshing one's memory since the previous request for specialized services, and the generally higher overheads naturally borne by a sophisticated administrative structure, all contributed to a massive expenditure that was necessary for the job it performed but ultimately wasn't reflected in the fee it was paid. (In mid-1978, over a year after the official opening, the Arup office was, like P & R, still working on Beaubourg and had a claim for an unpaid fee approaching £750,000. P & R was approximately breaking even.)

The battle between Piano & Rogers and Arup over the fee split was very serious while it lasted. There was a meeting in Genoa when Ahm, Happold, Piano, and Rogers considered taking a small boat into the Mediterranean for isolation while they fought to the finish. The Arup people were used to big-company tact, and they especially couldn't cope with Rogers when he got abrasive. Though Rogers wasn't as impressed by Arup's institutional solidity as the engineers themselves were and the client may have been, he badly wanted them. He acknowledged the organization's expertise, Rice's and Grut's brilliance, and Happold's influence: though Happold spoke little French, it was chastening to see that he was the one at a meeting whom everyone would listen to.

Whatever the conflicts, they could be resolved with a fair deal (the architects thought) and certainly could be forgotten later in the good spirit inspired by successful progress on Beaubourg. And whatever the economic disproportions that had to be provisionally suffered (the engineers thought), it was impossible to believe that those would go unremedied once a just nation came to recognize a brilliant job done.

A steel boss (which its designers called "the sputnik") connects screwed horizontal ties and diagonal cross-bracing members to the tip of a gerberette

5 The conduct of the job

Though expectations were high about employing a management contractor, GTM began very badly. First of all, unlike the situation in England at the same time where big contractors were taking on the relatively unrewarding task of management contractor to add luster to their names, GTM not only didn't know the task, they had no real reason to learn it since they didn't suppose they would ever need to do the same job again. The prestige of their company was just fine, and they wondered if they were doing harm to it with this bizarre scheme. French contractors never worked creatively with designers as they were supposed to do on Beaubourg. They completely took over and then normally griped about the architects' and engineers' lack of foresight and experience. At times it seemed pretty painful for GTM to be doing otherwise. Worst of all, one of the chief assistants to GTM's director absolutely couldn't bring himself to believe in the structural design and went around saying so at every opportunity.

On one occasion Bordaz sent for Lennart Grut, the senior structural designer on Beaubourg for Arup, because the highly incensed GTM chief was in his office. "Look, are you certain the design can be built, or is it actually impossible?" Bordaz asked Grut. Grut staunchly defended it. "But," interrupted the GTM chief, "can you guarantee one hundred percent that nothing will ever go wrong?" This disloyalty infuriated the design engineers, though they had to acknowledge GTM's duty to speak out if it had qualms. Many months later when the huge steel castings were actually being made, Gerry Clarke, by then the administrative head of the Arup Paris office, had lunch with this same GTM chief. Clarke said, "You still don't believe in it, do you?" "No," the GTM chief admitted, "I still don't believe it will work. It will never work."

Nevertheless, understanding was lacking on the design team's side too. GTM had the virtues of its defects. In a way it was correct that GTM should be apprehensive. And it was only behaving according to type, because normally the contractor gets sued for design errors in France. (The GTM chief finally admitted that he was unduly pessimistic.) Besides, GTM's employees were capable and willing to protect the design team from less responsible nay-sayers, and that was working well. Everyone else in the construction industry may have thought that the job looked ridiculous and unmanageable, but the design team's confidence was seldom shaken. This was mostly due to the hoped-for insulation provided by GTM, plus the undeniably effective isolation between the design team and their fellow professionals because of the language gap. In England or Italy their professional colleagues would have been scathing the minute things looked to be getting out of hand. Piano and Rogers and Arup remained isolated from demoralizing chumminess with other architects, engineers, and the whole building industry of France until they were on course with building what they wished. On this weird "don't confuse me with the facts" basis, their insularity and lack of normal contact in a foreign country kept their confidence up.

GTM delivered best where it knew its task best. M. Grassin, the managing director, was always very positive. The firm organized all the necessary cranes, mobile equipment, and deliveries to the site: "Some problem," Rice said in admiration. GTM's project manager Jean Thaury was pragmatic and straightforward, and it was he who began providing a cool interface between the design team and the French construction industry, a role that kept growing. Useful insularity notwithstanding, the design team needed to know how to manipulate the industry in order to build effectively, particularly with their demanding technological requirements. To manipulate it, they had to understand it on a very refined level—where skills lay, how materials got shipped, how labor participates, how orders are filled, where competition exists, where unskilled workers are used, or where there are only specialists in a craftsmanship tradition. If they knew which potential supplier was able to achieve good quality under all the restricting conditions (which is what they needed to know at every turn), they would be able to start putting together groups of suppliers to achieve the quality wanted overall. The manipulation would become an orchestration.

Orchestrating resources was especially crucial for the mechanical equipment. The structural steelwork, while very unusual, was at least a standard building industry problem, and a few obvious industrial giants might be able to take it on. But long-lasting and rugged equipment in the electrical, plumbing, and air conditioning fields was almost unknown. The only installations where it was normal were in refineries, ocean drilling platforms, nuclear generating plants, and the like, where ruggedness was essential but visual qualities were of scant importance. GTM was able to find the makers of such equipment and knew who might be able and willing to make necessary modifications.

The other main thing GTM succeeded at from the designers' point of view was, simply, to present designs to the construction industry as if they were unexceptional. Rice in particular saw that the prestige of the design team (by which he meant their effectiveness, not the applause they got) depended absolutely on a sort of confidence game, where contractors and suppliers had to believe this was a standard job, and they were being asked to do only standard things, which they could achieve. GTM made the really intractable tasks seem OK.

Apart from those preoccupations, there was GTM's central job. An average of over £1,000,000 of construction per month was to be carried out at Beaubourg from mid-1972 to November 1975—£45 million total, though 70 percent of it was to be built off site. (On a later project in Britain for Lloyd's of London, Richard Rogers found that he couldn't get British construction experts to consider anything beyond £500,000 worth per month, though they thought the French building industry was only slightly more efficient than the British.) In order to put up a structure where you design as you build, you need an organization on site of adaptable builders. Once early problems had passed, GTM proved to be just that.

The competition brief had proposed a three-year construction period when it specified the end of 1975 as the completion date for the project. In the autumn of 1971 a total project time of just over four years was indicated, including designing, with site work due to commence in 15 months. A December 1975 finish would have been viable only if the brief were frozen and all design variations avoided. Since this was hardly credible, the design team predicted that conventional design and revisions would result in an overall program of longer than six years, which allowed for two years in developing the design, preparing tender documents, and obtaining competitive bids for the total building work, followed by a construction period of more than four years.

Heated discussions with the client led to further studies of the building work program by the Arup project planning group in London. They were able to show that no matter what happened, construction alone would have to occupy more than three years. Though this was grudgingly accepted by the client, Arup for its part reluctantly had to accept that its immovable target for completion was December 1975, so design development had to telescope within the construction period. As the design team were busy finding places to live, adjusting to an expanding design brief, and starting to come to grips with complex building regulations and procedures at the end of 1971 (and no budget had yet been announced, though cost studies had been made), the prospect of preparing for a start of work in June 1972, when the first section of the site became available, was formidable. Of course, starting to build while still designing—a technique called "fast tracking"—was not in itself unusual, but it was rarely applied against such odds. It was going to be a race against time between drawings and construction. In the event, excavation actually began in March 1972—only eight months after the competition results were announced, and before a design was fixed for the building aboveground.

The fast-track schedule meant that inspiring confidence was a job that the design team couldn't put entirely on the shoulders of GTM. They couldn't point to their own experience either. Before the competition, the largest building Piano & Rogers had built had a value of under a million pounds, and even the solid Arup office was new to the European continent. The Beaubourg building work had to progress while the architects and engineers made administrative mistakes, corrected them, established a Paris office, and added to the team—while the client's confidence grew, if possible. It took at least two years before the latter happened. For the first two or three years, not even the team members' confidence in each other could be taken for granted. The scheme looked suspect too. Arup was worried, Piano and Rogers were depressed, the client was nervous; everyone behaved neurotically. "In every handshake you'd look for the dagger," said one architect. Relationships were brittle. The worst time was during the basement construction. However they tried to look at it, things were just going down into a hole. The fighting among the team members was exhausting. People were saying this building will take ten years; it will make the Sydney Opera House look simple.

Between the architects and engineers, stress was high at one level because of uncertainties, interference from client groups, and the drawn-out disagreement over fees and responsibilities; and at another level, it was high because they were slightly different kinds of people. In the architects' view, for instance, Arup seemed unable to get itself organized for three years. It sent in team after team, leader after leader, which kept rupturing the continuity. The Arup office seemed like a battleground strewn with bodies. To Arup, Piano & Rogers's casualness, informal communications, and personal relationships seemed dangerous. There were hundreds of trivial frictions. In the inflatable structure they were sharing as an office for a while at the side of the Seine, the temperature soared during the day. The architects put up with it, because it was an inflatable, by the Seine. The engineers thought the architects were out of their minds—it had no charm for them; it was just too hot. Work pressure was heavy. Happold and Rogers had a typical argument. Rogers said, "Give me eight options and I'll choose." Happold replied, "Richard, if I do eight options, I'll bloody well choose."

Tolerance vanished. Finally, with people at each other's throats, a likeable mechanical equipment engineer called Jim Hill said, "Look—I've been through something like this before on another crazy job. What we're going to do is hire a bus. And we're going to all get in it together, and for three days we'll live together out in the country, as they do at Esalen" (a then-famous California center for human relationships). So they hired a bus, and for three days almost all the members of the design team were together, with formal sessions of amateur "conflict resolution." Each explained what he or she was doing and complained about the others. An architect would say, "We're professional, what about you?" Then everyone made comments. The psychological insights were trivial, but feelings started to change, and afterward many agreed that it probably saved the situation.

The architects' group was deliberately kept as small as possible, to simplify communication and formal organization. There was never enough staff to allow work to be confined to the normal hours of a week, but the extra workloads concentrated knowledge and responsibility in the hands of fewer, key designers. They were well paid. Well-intentioned advice from outside led P & R to search fitfully for senior, very experienced architectural administrators and coordinators who could solve the team's problems in those areas at a stroke, but "experience

counts for not much in the end," as Piano said. After two years
the architectural staff settled down to about 20 young architects,
two secretaries, one part-time model maker, and one
printmaking man. Their average age was about 30. After the role
struggle of early days, six teams grew up, each with a leader.
These were substructure, superstructure, facades and galleries,
systems (partitions, floors, ceilings, lighting, etc.) and
audiovisuals, planning (space layouts) and furniture, and
IRCAM.

Following the initial suggestion of the Établissement Public, the
designers, clients, and advisors worked all together for most of
the job: from *Palais,* to inflatable *pneumatique,* to offices, to
Beaubourg itself; six offices in as many years. For a while there
was a plan to buy a Seine barge to work on—for months they
were designing the barge instead of the building, said Ahm—
but that never came about.

Under the pressure of time, the drawings, models, and reports
were minimized. Where necessary, the models were made by the
architects, apart from large display and publicity models.
Meetings and design conferences were plentiful. No draftsmen or
professional interpreters were used. Everyone was forced to speak
French when it was necessary to make contact. Though no one
remembers consulting any authorities on creative organization
and management, the team groped toward effectiveness through
seasoning alone. Team loyalty gradually grew strong. When
objectives conflicted, understanding and good relations were
always maintained within the design team at the expense, if
necessary, of understanding and good relations between the
design team and others (the Établissement Public and especially
the programmation team were relied on for diplomatic

communications, and to a lesser extent so were the management contractors). No doubt the same generally happens with the crew of a film, or the personnel of an army patrol. And the psychological pressures seemed to reduce notably once the building was aboveground. There was a dramatic change of heart and attitude in everybody. Things seemed to be really moving, and like the steel going rapidly up into the air, people's spirits suddenly started soaring.

The architects were deployed by building zones; the engineers by disciplines. The quantity surveyor team struggled along. Initially, the quantity surveyors attempted to computerize the cost control, but because of technical difficulties and special client requirements a suitable program could not be found. Most of the controlling process was manually executed. Every month, complete updated cost control statements had to be submitted to the client. To do this, the work at its peak was demanding constant attention by eight quantity surveyors, three of whom were English and five French. The largest control and cost problem was in mechanical equipment. After long discussion it was decided to form a group of contractors to carry out the work. Investigating the short-listed mechanical equipment contractors, the cost control QS team actually got access to their company books and assessed the amount of work they had handled in recent years to determine their general capability.

In the course of the job there were no fewer than seven Ministers of Culture who came and went, varying from sympathetic to antagonistic in attitude toward Beaubourg. A few members of the competition jury remained in regular evidence. Prouvé came by occasionally to advise on staff and so on, and he and Piano became good friends. Sandberg of the Stedelijk Museum sometimes visited and "gave crits," that is, discussed the designs with the architects. When Bordaz wanted to strengthen his hand during one crisis, he brought the jury back over to confirm that the Beaubourg team was going in the right direction.

There wasn't much for the jury to see. In a more conventional building, every element of the brief would have had its own space and enclosure. The developing brief of the programmation group might have required (but didn't) that the library should be so-and-so high, walls should be so far apart, and so on. Or the architects might have been planning to have every secretary's room located between the circulation space and the room of the head of department, and so on. It wasn't being done that way at all. Piano & Rogers refused to draw such prescriptive plans while the situation was fluid. Even Philip Johnson was surprised when he asked to see the plans and was told they didn't exist. P & R's working method kept the programmation group slightly worried. But Rogers and Piano both had had a lot of experience with open-plan offices and factories, and they knew that it would be wasteful to draw detailed plans until very late; it was only necessary to allocate approximate areas for various purposes. As for where somebody sat, or where the doors were, or where there might be toilets, it wasn't crucial to have hypotheses or interim answers. The answers appeared very far along in the process.

At least floor plan areas were sometimes sketched for the general allocation of building uses. A more remarkable and radical omission in the Beaubourg design procedure was the lack of real elevations, which were not done until nearly the end. The exterior view elevations that were kept for show, as Rogers, Piano, Rice, Barker, Grut, and a few others in the design team knew, were merely placebos, to be used for reference until all the information and design development became resolved into real forms. An overall framework had been created, and parts were continuously added within. Of course most people in the construction industry expect a building to be described by plans and elevations. The design team therefore had an Emperor's Clothes problem in trying to convince contractors and suppliers that they knew what they were doing, while they were actually soliciting help and leaving open most of the possibilities about what would be done. Because the elevation only emerged after the details were clear, at times the whole process of definition at Beaubourg seemed in reverse.[1] The practical drawings only identified where equipment could go, and then the team started working directly with manufacturers. They found it was really the only approach. Afterward, Rice in particular felt that the principal means they had to use to elicit performance was to convince contractors that the process was quite normal. Once hooked, they would start to see the problem the way the designers wanted. In these terms, the process of design lasted through all four years of construction as the design team became involved successively in different building elements.

The advanced technology of many parts of Beaubourg made practical decisions crucial. Usually in building design, a hierarchy of decision making starts with the designers and descends in various steps to the builders. Yet the contribution of the builders is always vital, and often it is more important than the contribution of the original designers, because to make something new, one must have someone who is willing to take

---

1 This does happen on certain kinds of modern buildings, though seldom utterly without a concept about the way things will finally look (a clutter of mechanical gadgets is not an utterly undefined conceptual "look" either).

the risk, state a price, and make it. Every element and every contract in Beaubourg was the subject of a fixed-price competitive tender, and once signed, there was no going back. The manufacturing risk rested with the subcontractor, and this often included the development of special details, in nonstandard situations, with unfamiliar materials. Though the design team tried hard to specify accurately at the tender stage what was required, information was often uncertain. Development afterward would be necessary. Teamwork with the construction industry was the only possibility for success.

The justification for this, as Rice put it later, is in the design of a machine such as a car. The quality of a car is not measured by how it looks in a side view—that's very minor (though, as a critic of this theory might feel obliged to say, its looks help sell it). The quality of a car for its makers, and for many buyers, is measured by the design of the components that go into it and the design of the various pieces in it (and finally, one might add to help along Rice's theory, the buyer's subjective experience, which, like that of a visitor to a building, is largely sequential and kinetic). Beaubourg was to be the same: the issue was the *resolution* of the composed elements. Near the beginning of the design development, the designers didn't know what those elements would be, where they would come from, how they would be made; and most of them would have to be very new because it wasn't usual to put things like switches and electric motors on the outside of a building.

In the vital relationship between Beaubourg's design and industry, an example of cooperation was the construction of the external elevators. Otis of France was the only contractor prepared to tender on the whole of the range of equipment required, including the external and internal escalators, so it was chosen. Though now common, exterior elevators were still rare in Europe in the early 1970s. It was clear to Laurie Abbott's group that they would have to adapt Otis's standard elevator for exterior use. However, at first the design team found it extremely difficult to get the right kind of information in order to analyze the standard elevator for their needs. Otis was baffled: an elevator was an elevator. After a number of visits to Otis's assembly plant, Abbott decided to consider that the cabin was really no more than a chassis frame with a box inside and various pieces of machinery mounted at the top and bottom. By isolating three elements—the cabin, the chassis frame, and the mechanical parts—it was possible to treat each separately.

The elevator cabin was redesigned by taking the standard cladding elements, turning them inside out, and using heavier gauge materials, with certain refined details provided at the corners. At first Otis wasn't sure why the changed elements were acceptable while the original elements were not. After one or two trial assemblies Otis grew excited by the possibilities of the altered design and began to recommend small extra improvements that could be carried out. The mechanical parts were then arranged on the chassis frame. Problems such as the movement of the entire elevator framework and supporting rails, which initially Otis had said did not move but which within a steel skeleton would inevitably deflect slightly, were handled by a gradual understanding of the problem on both sides. The result was that Beaubourg never risked the uncertainties of a brand new untested design; and Otis too had the benefit of the technological development.

Traveling maintenance cabs above pedestrian galleries on the west elevation

The team making up the client body, the Établissement Public set up by Pompidou, had most to do with the organization of work. Halfway through the job they numbered about 300, with programmation alone close to the size of the architectural team. This small army monitored the design team and contractors, was responsible for costs, and was finally accountable to the government and the public. Relations especially between the construction team (then headed by André Darlot) and the design team were not easy. Darlot was tough. The construction group had a natural suspicion of the way the non-French consultants worked, but the construction group itself had a tendency, the architects later alleged, to make every delay or minor disagreement into a full-blown crisis. It seemed necessary for them to have a major crisis every day.

The client construction group's most important role was as mediator between the design team and the statutory bodies with whom they had to deal. As novices in France, the design team had a very inadequate idea of which approvals were necessary and how they should be applied for. More particularly, they had no idea at all who would be making the official decisions. The role that the construction unit undertook was to interpret the partial decisions received from various meetings. This was particularly evident in meetings with the French fire safety authority, the CSTB, where there never seemed to the architects to be any progress. Each time a requirement was satisfied, the requirement appeared to change. In reality, of course, the CSTB situation in France was not so different from the state of affairs with administrative officials in other countries. When officialdom's human faces are not familiar and thus easily understandable, it is difficult to press forward.

The construction group's intervention was also to be important soon in arguing the acceptance of the steel structure tender design through SOCOTEC. SOCOTEC was the *Bureau de Controle* nominated to check the steel design and ensure that it satisfied French regulations and was an acceptable insurance risk. In the beginning, the SOCOTEC investigation team was extremely skeptical and felt the design was bizarre. However, with persistence and with the active and continuous support of the Établissement Public construction group, the design team was able to allay their fears one by one.

The burgeoning programmation group of at least ten people remained active enough for its size. Accommodation changes were always instigated by programmation. There were two reasons why the building volume seemingly changed between the competition scheme and the definitive scheme (for instance, filling in the open space between building and piazza). The early change was due to cost considerations limiting the open frame. The second was the absolute condition of an overall height not to exceed 42 meters, which emerged quite late. The pre-1956 historic height of Paris was 31 meters, and that is why the view from Beaubourg is over a flatscape of roofs. The new 42-meter limitation was not a programmation requirement or even a town planning requirement, but had to do with fire safety: the 28-meter height to the fourth floor was the highest that Paris fire truck ladders would reach (Beaubourg's present fifth floor functions as a terrace over the fourth, at least in terms of fire safety). Similar rules apply in towns of other countries. Anything above these determining heights was deemed a "high building," and there was no such thing as a Parisian high building to which the public could be admitted under the conditions anticipated— usually public buildings were only one or two stories high. Beaubourg eventually became the only building in Europe on such a scale having public access at all levels.

The effect of these changes on the overall building volume was nil, but the impression conveyed—especially to the architects, who were the most aware of and unhappy about them—was of a great increase in volume, since the ground floor and most of the other provisionally open volumes of the structure were filled in. It was simply the way the design evolved, in programmation's view; Lombard had never been friendly to the open space under the building. The only major addition to the brief was IRCAM, which anyhow was added in an adjacent separate site. Besides IRCAM, the overall spaces from the original brief to the finished building changed less than 1 percent, a credit to programmation's tight rein on spatial inflation.

Despite evident devotion and relative efficiency, among the architects there was disgruntlement about whether the programmation group's wonderful service was really a good thing. Piano and Rogers both were unconvinced. Programmation not only could have defended the brief but could have actively campaigned for the architects' beloved "nonprogrammed" areas, especially the piazza and facade activities. One of the problems was that beyond programmation's given role, it was always searching for others, instead of following the design team's lead. Its area of expertise—specifying a function that could be suited by a form—was exactly what it could use to justify its own administrative existence when necessary. The architects under pressure were only too pleased to have the programmers most of the time, since they could turn to the client and say, "Don't tell us, tell them." The architects would be off the hook, but they would pay for this by getting interpreted instructions. Was programmation therefore predigestion? A frequent criticism of architectural competitions is that the instructions are laid down and the architects must follow them, even if they don't agree with them and would reinterpret more creatively, given the chance; the case of a middleman programmation group seemed at times to have perpetuated such a situation right through the design development. When the clients got mad, they often didn't even get mad at the architects. (After some battles over responsibilities, programmation lost power. In 1975 they were largely replaced by a less efficient group, who got busy for a while specifying interiors and furniture.)

To the architects, the mission of the client sometimes needed uplift and refreshment, so at one stage Piano & Rogers delivered a lecture to them. The text was preserved, and the architects still believe it should be included in the whole story of Beaubourg's design. Here is the complete text in its original English:

> The image of culture is static and elitist; our problem is to make it live to both entertain and inform, not only for tourists or specialists, but for those who live in the neighbourhood, a neighbourhood in crisis. We must all participate, not as separate watertight departments either less or more elegantly organised, but as a total centre, a new experiment whose success or failure will affect us all. We must make contact and break down the suspicions surrounding culture. All standard operating procedures are on trial, no longer controlled by the rubric of some all-encompassing philosophy but by the pragmatic goad of new demands and the pressing need for workable alternatives. Our building and what is around is a tool, not a rigid tailormade architectural monument. It is fluid, flexible, easy to change, full of technical resources inside and outside, on top and underneath, but you and us, the users and the designers, must decide what to plug into those technical resources. It is our belief that the people of today and tomorrow, the curators, the specialists, the amateurs, must have the possibility of designing their own changing needs into the building, as far as possible freed from the limitation of the architectural form. We can study the areas in which change is most likely to happen, and by the use of modern techniques one can design in flexibility with movable partitions, walls, services, furniture and even structure.

> This in no way runs counter to producing a beautiful building. We accept that, supported by you as the users and programmers, the responsibility for integration and control down to the smallest detail must be ours, as we are the designers.

> The key to the satisfactory use of the building is not the number of square metres, but the usability of the space. It is, for example, internationally accepted that the use of a large open space can offer 10% to 25% more usable space than a more articulated, broken-up space. This can clearly be seen by analyzing the competition entries

of a number of existing buildings by such architectural masters as Aalto, Utzon, Rudolph, etc.

The equation of cost, time and control is misapplied by the consideration of short term objectives. To take the first, the capital cost of the centre is only a small part of the total cost when examined over ten years. Changes to interiors normally equal the total cost of the building within ten years. Ultra-violet heat gain through modern fully-glazed buildings can invalidate 15% of the circumference of the floor area; that can equal over 30% of the floor area in which one would not be able to hang paintings, put books, or work in. These problems could be mitigated by using more sophisticated and expensive internal organization at the time of construction. Air conditioning is expensive, but is needed to optimise the use of the building.

With air conditioning, one can create a more comfortable environment and increase the number of participants whilst also decreasing the cleaning costs of the building. By increasing robot control one would decrease the number of those needed to maintain the building. The annual salary bill for people employed in the centre after completion is likely to be 18% of the total building cost.

This is not the place to go into details, but we strongly believe that a rational assessment should be made of that equation: cost + time + control = value; and that it could be measured by mathematical techniques so that one could achieve a clear idea of the problem to be solved. This is another area the programmers could examine to ensure that we get maximum value for money.

We must not just accept the programme, but set up a system which analyses in detail the needs as related to our solution. The competition is now over and we must resist the tendency to narrow down and produce a simplistic architectural solution. Though the building may be simple, the use must be sophisticated and rich.

Those beautiful perfect programmation drawings show exactly what happens in each department, but who says there should be departments? Why should there be walls except perhaps to keep rain out and for security? We can control the environment: the acoustic with absorbent materials, with white noise and grey noise, with soft carpets and ceiling; privacy can be obtained by the use of lighting and screens on wheels. Why should the art books be in the library, and art solely in the museum? Why do we need an A1 reception? Can not all information normally offered here be on the facade, on the moving stairs, on the galleries, on the closed television system, on the dial-yourself videophone? Even external walls can be created by a warm air curtain and security achieved by alarm systems set off by changes in air pressure. Can all the facades, piazza and the roof be an extension of what goes on inside? Can we reproduce works of architecture, books, etc., on the facade; a different book per day in lights, with or without music?

The success of the centre depends both on the spectators and the users. The centre is a public event; thus the greater the public involvement, the greater the success. The centre must be organised for these events, for the old and the young, for the specialists and the amateurs, different activities for different occasions: walking, meandering, love-making, contacting, watching, playing, sleeping, passing, studying, skating, eating, shopping, swimming, summerland in winter and winterland in summer. Maybe the French electricity council and the water board could use part of the centre as a showroom to create a total environmental experiment.

We have new tools for entertainments for all ages and all people, such as space simulation, TV information retrieval systems, projector systems, television print-out systems from which we shall soon get our daily newspapers printed, and a vast variety of both objective and subjective participatory activities both old and new. The centre will act as a container of these goodies. For example, all services will be built into the piazza: pressurised air, electricity, heating, sound, etc. The facade of the building will contain tents and pneumatics which can be unfurled at a moment's notice in inclement weather; the piazza, as the building, must be used by the people: it is not designed just to aesthetically set off the building.

We believe that exciting things can happen when a variety of different activities meet. We believe that by overlapping activities and offering flexibility, one opens up the possibility of interaction outside the confines of institutional limits.

> One of our major concerns is that the non-programmed activities
> not backed by those programmation drawings without the support
> of specialists like yourselves, and without special budgets, will die,
> and with them the basic concept of the centre. You together with
> ourselves must specify the needs, and earmark the resources, and
> control the quality for the success. The failure will be the
> responsibility of all of us. Perhaps we should all be locked up in one
> room together so that we can really engage in a dialogue and try to
> achieve these goals.

A number of things might be concluded from Piano & Rogers's
text. It shows an admirable regard for the role of culture in a
democracy. It gives a cogent argument for a populist monument.
It has a perhaps less durable "arts lab" middlebrow attitude,
characteristic of the early 1970s and noticeable particularly
among mass media people and architects of that age, whose
concern for cultural expression could be shown by suggesting
that books could be projected on a building's facade and its
piazza might contain pressurised air for inflatables that could be
blown up at a moment's notice. Finally, one reads it with a sense
that the client auditors must have already heard it many times
before, might have come up with some of these very ideas
themselves initially, and perhaps were beginning to feel badgered
about having to excuse themselves to the design team for
refusing to extend the building's brief. When they refused, they
doubtless did so for some good reasons, as well as for some crass
and unworthy ones.

It was hard to know whether or not such consciousness-raising
propaganda efforts were helpful in the end, but the design team
kept trying.

• • • • •

On the engineering front, decisive refinements were under way.

The gerberette refinement: Continuing economy problems on the main steelwork made the Arup engineers explore various truss girder designs for the big horizontal members. There was the Vierendeel truss girder of the 1971–72 APS initial scheme, but that was interim and unsatisfactory. A Warren truss girder of the revised APS scheme was better, but still subject to improvement.

The engineers were also conscious of the illogic of having a pair of columns in line at each end of the girders. Architecturally, these bracketed the exterior circulation and mechanical equipment zones, but structurally, the twinning seemed meaningless. If the truss girder carried beyond the first column, what was that column supposed to be doing? If the truss girder was supported by the first, what was the second column doing? The big conceptual break came in April 1972 when the structural engineers studied the possibility of putting all the compressive load on the inner columns and having the outer verticals in tension, pulling down. Between the two, and projecting past the inner columns toward the center, would be a cantilevered beam. This would shorten the girder, reduce the amount it would bend, and therefore allow a shallower, more lightweight, and cheaper girder design. If the truss girder rested on the inner point of the cantilevered beam, the beam could be detailed as a rocker arm. These cantilevered beams got to be called gerberettes in homage to a German engineer who had used this principle widely.[2]

---

2 This was Heinrich Gerber, 1832–1912, who was granted a German patent in 1866 for the design still known in mainland Europe as the Gerber girder, though in Britain and the United States it is called the cantilever girder. Gerber applied it as a continuous girder over several bridge spans with hinged joints and used this principle in many bridge designs. The Firth of Forth rail bridge is a famous version of the type.

View down from the glazed bridge between escalators and the building. In the most significant advance that refined the structural design, cantilever beams, called "gerberettes"—the structural elements with the large holes—were added to make up the span between what had formerly been a pair of columns bracketing the pedestrian galleries. The outer columns became tension ties, and the gerberettes were designed to pivot at the inner columns —one is shown here—to avoid placing lopsided ("eccentric") loads on them, which would have required the columns to be much more massive to counteract bending

Until the gerberette refinement, the structural engineers had been riding beyond the edge of practical building technology, but reduction of bending on the main girders meant that the necessary metallurgy and welding technology came within the current state of knowledge. This was a relief. And with the girder able to reduce in depth because of the action of the gerberettes, further progress on the exact form of truss girder was possible. One previous design had solid billets of steel for the chords of the trusses, but the rectangular dimensions of its members were so slender that the girder would have looked overfragile (and would have had to be supported laterally with more steel from girder to girder). After more experimenting with sizes, it was decided that the top and bottom chords of each truss and end struts should be done as paired hollow cylinders instead of individual fat cylinders. The horizontal double tubes side by side would visually appear more stable. It was planned that the cylinders would be centrifugally cast, to have different wall thicknesses where required. The main columns too (later to become the largest centrifugally cast tubes in the world when they were made) were designed to look extremely slender for the loads carried. Besides the gerberettes and tubes, casting would also be used for other complex steel parts, such as truss girder joints.

The Arup engineers were trying to "express" the elements by these means to provide an aesthetic lesson in structures, and they well realized that the visual importance of the building made refined steel detailing imperative. But they were determined to apply their expressive efforts strictly within the context of contributing to the most practical and economical steel structure for a building where, finally, each floor would be 170 by 48 by 7 meters without any fixed support inside.

Cafe terrace on the top level. The truss girders (typical ones are shown here) were designed with pairs of cylindrical chords top and bottom to reduce the structural mass that would have seemed more apparent with single, thicker chords. As at other external terraces, the structure continues above and around, allowing for future additions to and subtractions from the building envelope

The outside escalators: The process of clarifying and defining Beaubourg's technology most materially affected its looks in the case of the outside escalators. The competition design showed all main circulation between floors taking place on the outside of the building. During the design development—even though it was thought that some important vertical movement might happen inside too—this notion of outsideness grew to have major significance.

The escalators were considered by the designers to be crucial. It was felt that they should serve the whole main facade, animating the surface and making all floor levels true streets in the air. The escalators were thought of as Victorian recreation piers, in a modern version. Like them, they would encompass an eventful trip toward the horizon and back. Or, with their slopes and unobstructed views, they could fulfill the function of urban ski lifts, with that kind of gaiety and excitement. Whatever the comparison, they would be a key Beaubourg experience since nearly everyone would use them.

The design development headed toward a clearer version of the original idea. The revised APS scheme reduced the escalator routes from three to two, and the elevators were fairly central on the facade, all of which seemed good. But the *dual* escalator branches then seemed to pose an unnecessarily awkward choice to users.

In the Centre's functional planning, the main public activities were to be at the top and bottom, with the less active offices and library in the middle. Though everything was flexible and ultimately even the escalators could be altered, this need for movement between the two busy extremities was fixed upon as a main rationale for the building design. It then occurred to the design team that there would be no problem of user choice in *one* escalator route; it would consist of just a single, powerful diagonal, a mechanised *promenade architecturale*. Central elevators could also be sacrificed in order to achieve the strongest possible circulation directive. Mass movement would become a unified progression for all, without the confusing intermediate decisions of turns and branches. The chosen route would preferably go up

Gerberette pivot, with transverse ties connected through the pivot. In assembly, the gerberettes were lowered onto the columns rotated 90° horizontally, so the top and bottom holes were made elliptical to bypass higher pivots and the side holes were widened to allow the gerberette to turn once it was aligned with its own pivot

toward the south—toward the Seine and the view over Nôtre-Dame. The slowness of escalators would allow time to view Beaubourg and its city. As you climbed, the designers thought, you would just want to stay on—as Paris dropped away below you.

• • • • • •

With the definitive structure, circulation, and building zones set, the documents were finally able to be prepared for the steelwork bids, and these were sent out to some of the largest French firms. In mid-April 1973 the tenders came back and plunged the job into a grave crisis. The prices were about 60 percent higher than the quantity surveyors had calculated they should have been.

With a fixed budget, there was no way a 60 percent increase could be considered on steelwork, an item that itself was about a quarter of the total budget. Moreover, the overall prices tendered were very close to each other, and some subordinate prices among rival bidders were identical. It was a terrible thing to have to contend with. It was terrible not because the bids were merely high—but because the pioneering nature of the design made them seem not completely silly. In a way, the budget was the least of it: it was the challenge to control.

There was no proof of collusion, but Arup decided it was better to throw out all the tenders and seek others than just to submissively assume the figures were coincidentally very high and very close. To do otherwise, they thought, would have meant losing the respect of bidders on every contract to come, and perhaps even to have the professionals appear to be colluding themselves— assuming that paying for higher costs on the job would have even been possible. The crux of the matter was that *the appearance* of collusion would have been as bad as a real tendering ring. Being sure the client accepted the significance of the problem was very important in order to safeguard all further contracts on Beaubourg. Happold, Ahm, Rice, and Brian Watt of Arup went to talk to Bordaz and quickly persuaded him of this. A couple of hours after receipt, Bordaz declared the bids invalid. He was prepared to allow the design team to propose alternatives, but he warned them he could only defend them from the storm for a short time.

The pressure was acute, since the design team reckoned that failure to come up with an economic solution would mean no job; at least no design of theirs. The two lowest French tenderers continued to be negotiated with, because they lobbied the Minister of Production heavily—the 1973 economic slump was underway, and work was getting scarce. While the furthest thing from the minds of anyone in the design team was abandoning steel and resorting to a concrete structure, Grut and Rogers roughed one out for its terrifying effect on the steel contractors, and leaked news of it to the construction industry via the management contractor. It shocked a few design team members who were in the dark about its bogus purpose, because the GTM director's hostility to the steel design still rankled, and this kind of reckless disregard of design principle seemed all too characteristic of the Bureau d'Etude independence they had once feared. But the deception turned out to be a sophisticated and effective ploy. French steel makers had recently lost a number of big jobs to concrete structural alternatives, and perhaps they had good cause to be nervous about overreaching in the Beaubourg tenders. While Grut, Rogers, and GTM used a whiff of concrete to try to bring them to heel, the Arup office tried the more positive alternative of seeking interest from any other major steel makers. Krupp in Germany and Nippon Steel of Japan were soon very interested, and at the right sort of price. Arup realised that control of the design was probably saved.

Months of confidential negotiations subsequently led to the elimination of the Japanese firm, mainly on logistical grounds. But talks with Nippon Steel kept going to govern the Krupp negotiations. Finally, a secret contract was drafted with Krupp for the steelwork, within the original budget. The design was saved. It was also heartening that GTM had proved completely loyal to the design team at the crucial time. It was under tremendous pressure by French contractors at every point, and never more than just then. It insisted that the *Institut de Soudure,* the most respected controlling authority in France, be given the power to approve all actions taken on the steel design; but with representatives of the Institut present, GTM was freed from worry about claims that decisions were unfairly manipulated, and it acted unimpeachably.

The secretly negotiated Krupp figure was presented to the Établissement Public for approval. To the amazement of the design team, within hours one of the original French bidders offered a reconsidered tender price that was 1 percent less than the secret deal. All parties conducted staff purges to try to find out where and how the information leak had occurred. But Bordaz's decision was exemplary: he rejected the revised French offer and awarded the contract to Krupp, together with Pont à Mousson. The latter was a superb steel-casting contractor, and as a French affiliate of Krupp, it would provide a nationalist figleaf.

Happold was feeling the strain of the job. The misjudgment over his own firm's contract was a burden, and the steel problems didn't help. Though for the lack of a contract with the client he was as much to blame as anybody, he was getting fed up. He was adept at organizational infighting, even nimble, but he had some committed antagonists at Arup. Besides, he had a great deal of work waiting at Structures 3, and he didn't want to live in France. The London Arup office suggested he concentrate on Mideast work for a while. Happold became indignant and told colleagues he had been sacked from Beaubourg. This may not have been strictly the case, but after early 1973 he didn't return to Paris as an active job leader.[3]

---

3 Happold later founded his own practice, Buro Happold Consulting Engineers, and became head of the School of Architecture and Building Engineering, University of Bath. In December 1993 he was knighted for services to engineering and architecture.

Peter Rice, Lennart Grut, and Tom Barker were the key Arup design team members who stayed on Beaubourg. Since Rice was principal structural engineer on the world's most advanced steel architectural structure, his full capacity was required for the duration of the job. Other abilities notwithstanding, superlative work in structural design was what the client particularly expected from Arup, and this had to be justified. The Arup senior partners' decision was that Brian Watt, previously of their South Africa office, who had helped persuade Bordaz about rejecting the steel tenders, would run Beaubourg politically and managerially. Rice, anxious to do other work too, agreed at first that for six months he would stay in Paris and get over the technological hurdles until the steel structure was settled. The hurdles took a year, by which time Watt was ready to pack it in, following Happold. Rice realized that to have got as far as he had and then to depart with Watt would be another source of danger to design intentions. He decided to stay no matter what the administrative upheavals, and his contribution proved crucial. Thus Rice, not by inclination an administrator, floated upward to become one. To spare him the worst of it, Arup paired him with Gerry Clarke, leaving the structural design to Rice and Grut. Rice ceased having anything more to do with other work at Arup's London office from that point until the Beaubourg job was over.[4]

• • • • •

4 The chronology of Arup administrators was as follows:

July 1971–June 1972: Control from London through Happold, Barclay, Rice, Ahm.

June 1972– July 1973: Control in Paris (Watt, then Rice) with supervision from London (Ahm, Happold).

July 1973 to end: Complete control in Paris (Clarke, Rice), responsible to Ahm, the senior partner, in London.

The heavy cross-bracing members for the gerberettes nearest to the ground at each end of the building have their hinge pins held by cast stirrups. They were designed this way because not enough metal could otherwise be delicately incorporated into the connection. Bearing surfaces were made of harder alloys. The detailed design of these elements was worked out between the structural engineers and the foundry contractors

Fast tracking is an operation that can make one prematurely gray, since it assumes hierarchical design consistency, something not ordinarily to be expected in a complex design process. While the superstructure and even administrative problems at Beaubourg were being successively unsettled and resettled, the excavation and substructure, which had to be under way in order to finish the job on time, was fast tracking ahead.

The concrete substructure had five different levels with a total floor area on the order of 65,000 square meters including roadways. It comprised roughly 48 percent of the built volume of Beaubourg, it was to get its own artificial environment, and it was all the more impressive for having been started before any definitive drawings were done for the building above. Its design was under the team leadership of Walter Zbinden, in association among the engineers with John Morrison at the beginning and later with Rob Pierce. Zbinden, a Swiss architect, attracted a few other Swiss and north Europeans (other design team members pretended to outsiders that the Swiss were French).

The basement as built went down to a depth of 19 meters over fairly extensive areas. Since the water table lay about 10 meters above that, there was an uplift problem in times of flood—the whole basement, or rather the slabs with all they carried, was subject to being driven up by hydraulic force. Resisting natural uplift of six to ten tons over a surface of about 19,000 square meters would have been very expensive. On the other hand, fortunately this was only water, not béarnaise sauce. The solution arrived at by Zbinden's team was to place horizontal drains beneath the slab that were linked to reservoirs, from where the water if any would be constantly pumped into sewers. In case of pump failure, there were reservoirs designed to have a one-day capacity. After the reservoirs filled, the water would overflow to fill the lowest building volume, which was estimated to have a three-day capacity. After that, manhole covers in the ground slab would lift and water would flow into the basement, but by that time the ministerial cars and tour coaches would have presumably been shifted.

An equally serious substructure risk was "heave." Unlike uplift by water, heave distinguishes unwanted movement of a plastic kind. This might well occur in béarnaise sauce, but it is usually found in the soil pressure of clay. If parts of clay are pushed down by intense loads, other less-loaded parts might heave, or push up. Heave was anticipated at Beaubourg, and the problem was solved with appropriate expansion joints in the concrete, with the great concentrated loads carried down to the soil supported by "barrettes": discrete concrete walls carrying down to a limestone stratum. Barrettes and basement were designed by Arup engineers to move independently, if move they did.

Because critical path analyses had shown that it was crucial to start construction of the superstructure as early as possible, a temporary retaining wall was constructed, technically known as a "Berlinoise" type. The Berlinoise wall allowed rapid placement of steel supports, and excavation work, to continue independently.

The substructure was not only vital as structure; it was the place where much of the technological and mechanical backup for the building above was to be. It was also the place where all Beaubourg's contract procedures were tested to indicate the competence of the designers, the control of construction on the site, and the quantity surveyors' pricing accuracy—and these were all successfully proven.

A critical insurance matter then arose. The decision to
deliberately allow water to penetrate the building if necessary in
order to reduce uplift put the matter of waterproofing severely
into question. The resolution of the problem was eccentrically
dictated. The choice of waterproofing of the basement, in theory,
needed to depend on prior decisions about what was and wasn't
important. Car park areas, for example, which would be
permitted to flood after due warning, didn't need waterproofing.
But building insurance, not design logic, was determining such
decisions. In France the insurance of a building was covered by a
renewable 10-year guarantee provided by the collective
Groupement des Entreprises (GECO) and was accepted for insurance
and controlled by *Bureaux de Controle,* or checking authorities.
The checking authority enforced conformity with official practice
recommended in the *Document Techniques Unifié* (DTU). In
waterproofing matters, GECO proved particularly strict in
insisting that only recognized and approved materials be used,
and that their application be entirely according to DTU
standards. This inevitably meant a process was given either a
green light or a red one: something was either accepted to be
waterproof, or it wasn't. With no concept of partial
waterproofing acceptable to the authorities, French clients had to
decide for themselves whether they wanted a waterproof
building or didn't. Beaubourg's client accepted technical
arguments put forward by the design team for a partial solution.
While the cost savings were substantial, Beaubourg (except for
IRCAM, where a total waterproofing solution was adopted)
thereby lost the possibility of insurance offered by GECO.

Though there had been a small uproar in the French steel
industry after the steel contract was awarded to Krupp, everyone
working on Beaubourg was cheered by the outcome. They were

Part of the east elevation. The "functional" rather than "designed" look was deemed a just and reasonable system of representation at Beaubourg, where (as in other modern buildings) ventilation equipment is likely to be replaced or altered over a relatively short period of time convinced that nothing could stop them from then on. Prior to erection, Krupp seemed to be getting on well. But then a crucial mistake was discovered. It happened through overly glib assumptions, or, as they are sometimes called, "communication problems." Mainly as a result of these, Krupp wound up with a quite small profit margin, and Pohlig, which made many of the castings, took a financial beating.

When the castings specification was written for the contract, Arup had used the latest available technical information to describe the steel quality needed. This came from practice in the nuclear reactor industry, on big steel pressure vessels being made in the United States and Britain, on space program standards developed in the United States and France, and on North Sea oil rig standards laid down in Britain. These techniques were in the esoteric field of fracture mechanics. The steel contract called for the performance of the metal to meet a British Development Standard (BDS), which described the quality wanted. Its basis was a procedure that had to be followed, testing a sample to destruction. The critical thing was the ability of the material to hold in check cracks that would appear when under stress. One had to test under certain "crack growth" conditions at certain temperatures to find out if crack growth was adequately arrested, and this had to be related to the ability of detecting the actual flaws ultrasonically. Both had to be dealt with in parallel. A satisfactory material would be one with flaws that, measured under the control conditions, were smaller than the flaws the material could tolerate under the control conditions.

To use the BDS, one had to read and understand it, then follow it with tests. In order to give contractors immediate guidance for pricing purposes, some more conventional *reference* values were given, known as Charpy values. Krupp was pressed for time, and the unforeseen effect of Arup's helpfulness in giving reference values was to have the contractors ignore the complex performance standard, the BDS, and only to make the materials capable of meeting the elementary Charpy v-notch test. The inexactness that might have been caused would have been bad enough. The real trouble was that Krupp set about getting superior quality the wrong way. Instead of making the material less brittle, they made it more strong (two quite different metallurgical qualities). The material was made to contain chromium, molybdenum, and titanium, instead of what it should have had, which was nickel. The resultant costly alloy was actually worse than ordinary mild steel in terms of the standards. It failed all the proper tests. Many parts had been cast by then, and scrapping them was no longer a reasonable option if progress was to continue and Krupp was to be motivated to proceed. It was decided that the parts should be reheated and cooled to achieve extra tempering, which went on in October and November 1973, less than a year before erection. They still weren't ideal after that treatment (heat treating isn't very satisfactory on thick steel, especially cast steel, because some zones of the material don't ever get the proper crystal transformation). Rice and Grut were unhappy about the imperfections. Krupp had said it understood the design requirements, but it didn't understand, because of a language problem or something of that sort, and it hadn't been aware that it didn't understand.

The misunderstanding with Krupp was very unfortunate, but it was the most extreme communication problem of the building process, and it was still a retrievable error. Elsewhere the Babel of languages had no obvious Tower of Babel effect. Krupp otherwise did everything expected of it. It took commendable care of the biggest requirement of Beaubourg: detailing and erecting the "primary steel," the main structural members. Krupp's shop drawings had to confirm the precise form the steelwork was to take. The steel members had to be thought about in terms of easy erection and quick assembly on site. Detailing all the parts in an exacting manner later made it possible for Krupp to put up 1,500 tons of steel a month in the center of Paris—an exceptional achievement.

• • • • • •

Not since the one occasion of the competition announcement had the design team met Président Pompidou. His apparent illness hadn't seemed to concern them directly. Suddenly, his death was announced on April 2, 1974, and Valèry Giscard d'Estaing became president of France in early May.

Giscard was not of the Gaullist party like Pompidou. His regime, whatever its merits, seemed to have arrived at the worst possible time for Beaubourg. Though the steel specification crisis had been overcome, delivery and erection still hadn't occurred. As yet, very little was visible on site to do mute public relations for the job; only the excavation and basement levels were evident. Public relations was definitely needed. To the design team, and even—if they were reading the hints correctly—to the Établissement Public, it appeared all too likely that the project would be cancelled, regardless of wasted expense. Not only was there a new politician and a new party, but a new set of cultural advisors, with their own objectives to achieve. Who could expect them to continue supporting a building that everyone was calling a monument to Pompidou, which cost a major part of the national budget for the arts, had a lot of internal problems, was slammed by the press, attacked by part of the French architectural profession, and hated by the public for causing the ruin of a beautiful area of Paris?

And it was being run by foreigners too. Just before Giscard took over, M. Lemaret, the respected head of the modern art museum, had resigned (some said because of his opposition to Beaubourg), to be replaced by Pontus Hulten, a Swede. At that juncture there were engineers with a Danish firm name, British and Italian architects, the Germans doing steelwork, and a Swedish museum head. "It sure isn't a popular project," even Rogers admitted. Cancelling it seemed an easy way for a politician to pick up a few hundred thousand votes. Moreover, Les Halles next door was in a hotbed of trouble. Its famous market structures had been demolished under Pompidou—an appalling decision—and the redevelopment of Les Halles was linked in everybody's mind to Beaubourg.

So Giscard, three months after coming into office, called in Beaubourg and Les Halles for examination. To the defensive Établissement Public, it brought to mind the circumstances surrounding the Les Halles demolition a few years before. Then, with official approval, a gang had started tearing down the pavilions designed by Baltard the first week in August when people were away and there was no one to fight it; here it was the beginning of August again, and this time two big schemes might quietly be stopped by the officials. Piano, Rice, and other key Beaubourg people were away. Giscard refused to see any of Beaubourg's design team, or Bordaz. Panic seized everyone. The new Giscard cabinet's decision was to consider only the one main architectural model. It was rumored that Bordaz would be dismissed; he himself told friends he expected it. Meanwhile Rogers and Lombard went to see the Minister of Culture, which was all they could do. He was uninformative. Piano and Rogers conferred by phone and threatened to resign if Bordaz was dismissed. Arup produced an expenditure report showing that around 80 percent of Beaubourg's cost had already been contracted. Its message was that it was about two months too late to stop the project.

After a short but horrible period of agony and despair, the first peep of news the design team received was a telephone call from Giscard's secretary. Bordaz rang soon after with a more detailed message from the Élysée Palace. The Les Halles redevelopment was going to be radically cut—but Beaubourg was not. It had been a close shave, he said. The factors that had helped Beaubourg were guessed by the rejoicing team: Giscard's political debt to the Gaullists, whose votes he needed; Bordaz's effective advocacy; the design, on its merits; and the brief, on its merits, including the fact that the programmation group was able to defend the project with mountains of paperwork on studied social requirements that were difficult to assail. Still in high spirits the next morning, Rogers asked Bordaz for full details. Bordaz said, Actually, they did make one or two stipulations. Remove all the visible mechanical service equipment from the exterior. Lower the building by one floor. And cut IRCAM's budget by a third. It was a complete disaster after all! To Rogers, everything seemed finished. The design team hardly slept for four days writing further defensive reports.

IRCAM is short for the *Institut de Recherches et de Coordination Acoustique/Musique.* Mike Davies was its Piano & Rogers design team leader. Taking form from instructions by Pierre Boulez, the director nominated by the government, the Institut had grown ambitiously in concept, until the underground (for soundproofing) building for the study of acoustics and music had become known as "Petit Beaubourg," vying seriously with "Grand Beaubourg." IRCAM's first bold brief had been to make it the world's preeminent center for musical technology. It was to have electro-acoustic studios, advanced computers, acoustical research laboratories. It was also to be given experimental sound chambers ranging from anechoic chambers (with almost no measurable sound reverberation, like a windless desert), to an *Espace de Projection* big enough to hold 500 people, where by changing walls, volumes, and surfaces, almost any sort of performance chamber could be created. IRCAM was to have five underground levels with a glass roof, public access to much of it via elevators and a grand foyer, and conference rooms, a library, and studios for musical researchers from all over the world. Excavation was down to almost three of the levels. Unfortunately for Petit Beaubourg, it had started later than Grand Beaubourg, and most expenditure hadn't yet occurred.

The Giscard demands were disastrous, but, apart from the IRCAM cut, they were mostly impractical at that late stage. Money certainly wouldn't be saved: 80 percent of the value of all contracts had been committed, as Arup had pointed out. The building was being constructed in two-floor braced sections, so removing one floor was inadvisable. And where would the lost space go? A report with cautionary findings was prepared. As for the mechanical service equipment, if Giscard really didn't want to see it, it could be covered by louvers, or whatever he wished, after the building was completed; the structural design was capable of taking such extra loadings. There would be fire problems with it, but it could be done. The government would just have to provide the extra money.

Negotiations with the Élysée Palace left things at that. When the dust from the political upheaval settled, the top floor and the mechanical services were going to stay more or less as designed.

Smaller changes were to be made: all the complex-looking cleaning and maintenance equipment on the roof was not to appear (and was mostly omitted from the job after that), but the major air handling equipment was left alone. The elevator towers were to be made lower so as not to project so much above the structure.

Within a month, the steel structure began to roll up. In fact it had been ready for delivery when Giscard reviewed the project, but Krupp had decided to hold off putting the erection crew on site until after the August holidays.

The brightly painted mechanical equipment on the east elevation has a supergraphic effect seen from the fast-moving traffic of the Rue de Renard. If the mechanical equipment had been painted all grey or beige, Beaubourg would have seemed plain industrial architecture, instead of communications architecture

6 Crises, panics, and smooth going

Beaubourg's construction was a tremendous enterprise, but it occurred mainly in factories and workshops far from the site. Few individual impressions of the effort at the time would have given a sense of the entire process, because there were so many makers, suppliers, and skills—two or three times as many as in an ordinary modern building. This multiplication of elicited talents and efforts, an outgrowth of Piano & Rogers's and Arup's research-and-development-mindedness, characterized their design method and professional style.

From the drafting room to the building site, a typical element might have been realized like this. The architect or engineer would first identify the need and, from the generality of similar needs, isolate the one that could be met by a particular branch of industry—for example, a mechanical ventilator control could be isolated from the generality of duct or wall or window devices. Learning from the team leader that no similar devices had already been designed or selected, the designer could check with the fire and other authorities to learn the standards that applied, if he or she didn't know already. Then the designer would be able to get aid from GTM to find suppliers of such a device, if necessary. If there were no existing suppliers and the device had to be an invention or a hybrid of several devices, GTM could advise on makers who might be interested in developing the device along the lines laid down in the architect's or engineer's "performance specification." This was a descriptive brief—in words, pictures, or both—specifying what the device had to do and stating any other requirements, such as materials, colors, or durability. Either way, the designer would begin having illustrated consultative exchanges with the potential manufacturer or manufacturers, getting criticism on the original design proposal if necessary. From these, it might emerge that only one maker had the right idea, and a contract would be negotiated with that one. Or several potential makers offering acceptable options might remain in cost competition. (The quantity surveyors would be advising at this stage, and the client would be consulted before the maker was actually chosen.) When chosen, the maker would usually be asked for detailed design drawings, known as "shop drawings," which would be checked by the design team member before the fabrication of the exemplary mechanical ventilator control. To the extent that anything at Beaubourg was typical about the construction and could represent it all, it wasn't the site labor, swinging of cranes, or even the rapidly rising structure, but it was this process of eliciting things from suppliers in a responsive way, with parties both behind and beyond the drawing board taking part creatively.

With few exceptions (mainly that of the underground construction), sitework was assemblage—that was the theory. This commitment to the assembly of prefabricated parts wasn't only a matter of design ideology, though with Piano & Rogers it was that too, but was a matter of increasing speed on site. Prefabrication was intended to be the smooth coming-together of what had already been thought out carefully in advance via the drawings, specifications, consultations, and contracts. Of course sitework at Beaubourg remained demanding: it meant meeting extreme challenges, finding shortcuts. In a lot of areas the work called for exploiting the limit of existing technology, within a killing time schedule, under absolute control of costs. Administratively, there were no specialist sitework architects, though Bernard Plattner worked mainly on site. Each team leader carried through from initial design to final product in one area of responsibility. And prefabrication notwithstanding, to build Beaubourg on site took an army of workers. Sometimes there were contending armies at stages where too much had to happen in too brief a time, such as just before the opening. Off the field were the staffs and logistics of supply. Beyond them was French industry, and beyond that, international industry. The rate of Beaubourg's spending on construction alone put it in the league of France's greatest economic commitments of the time.

As workers in typical British construction gangs were Irish and in America were native American, Irish, or black, in France the laborers were typically Algerians; Beaubourg was an Algerian achievement as much as a French and a British-Italian one. Krupp was expected to be diplomatic about its German presence, but within weeks of its being given the steel contract, the friendly *bidonville* of ramshackle contractors' huts already on site was eclipsed by a phalanx of Krupp huts, parallel and bright blue. Tall German engineers arrived with blue helmets and uniforms with Krupp badges. The client issued instructions, and Algerian workers were detailed to paint out the word "Krupp" as each steel piece arrived. In time, the Germans in their turn were outnumbered and gave way to other squads, regiments, and armies as construction specialty overlapped construction specialty. So site work and assemblage progressed.

· · · · · ·

Since in principle the structural steel design had been conceived as a giant construction toy kit, each element was to connect to its neighbor in a simple way, and pieces could be shipped individually. But since site welding was to be avoided in general, and always avoided in tension locations, some pieces had to be big. The largest were the truss girders, the main horizontal members. A scheme had been presented by Arup showing how these could be transported to Paris by barge and moved to the site as a *convoi exceptionnel*. The entire erection was conceived around this. But in the event, Krupp chose to bring the truss girders by rail from Germany and then move them to the site by road.

Between midnight and dawn on designated nights, the site was open to receive the delivery of steel elements from Germany. Starting from September 1974, three girders arrived each week, usually on a Thursday night. Beaubourg's columns, the almost equally sizeable vertical elements, were delivered in two pieces each.

The steel structural frame was then erected one bay at a time. Starting with a tower crane standing at one end, three such bays of columns, gerberettes, and truss girders were built before the tower crane itself had to be moved. The floors, of concrete cast in place atop preassembled reinforcement and formwork sections, followed one bay behind the steelwork. To complete the superstructure, bracing was put in after the initial "dead load" of the floors—mainly concrete—had been applied.

The time necessary to erect one bay was ten days, and the whole steel frame erection, including concreting of the floors, took eight months. As all the metal detailing was simple and bold in order to be visibly understandable afterward, the erection of these deliberately explicit pieces was fast and without major problems. It meant that, though the steel production in the foundry had been troublesome, the steel reaching the site was able to be put up just in time for the arrival and addition of the mechanical equipment components. The quick, trouble-free erection retrieved time losses in the whole program.

TECHNICAL NOTES ON THE STEEL STRUCTURE[1]

The principal structure consists of 11 identical internal steel frames and two end-braced gable frames, making 13 bays in all. Each bay is 12.8m wide, giving an overall length to the building of 166.4m. Each of the

---

1 This is an edited version of notes by Ove Arup and Partners.

Construction of Beaubourg, late spring 1975

standard internal frames consists of two compression columns 48m apart, two tension ties a further 6m outside on both sides, making 60m overall, and two cantilever beams called gerberettes supporting a truss girder spanning 44.8m on each of six floors. The basic frame is free to rotate at the points of support of gerberette-column and truss girder–gerberette. Ground floor (piazza level) height is 10.5m, and other floor-to-floor heights are 7m. The gable frames at either end are braced beam-to-beam and to the ground, transmitting horizontal transverse wind and stability forces to the ground. Each floor, which spans 12.8m beam-to-beam, transmits these horizontal forces from end to end of the building. The floors act as horizontal beams between gable frames. Despite floor sections partially missing on the higher levels, at least 65% of the lateral depth of floors is always acting as a beam.

Longitudinal wind and stability forces are transmitted to pre-tensioned cross-bracing, placed 0.5m outside the tension ties. This cross-bracing has horizontal members at every second floor—the 2nd, 4th, and 6th. The tension tie is the third member in the system, and acts together with the bracing to provide stability. There is more bracing than required, and the Xes are therefore omitted where access to the building is necessary. Cross-bracing connects to floor slabs by horizontal bracing at even floors. At odd floors, the compression columns only are connected to floors and each other. Tension and compression of columns and ties generated by the modified Gerber system transfer directly into the subsoil mass without touching the basement structure.

There are no expansion joints within the superstructure. All temperature distortions, either between adjacent floors, between the outside and inside facades, or between the building and the structure below it, are either absorbed by the flexibility of the members, or resisted by their stiffness.

COLUMNS are centrifugally cast steel tubes made by Pont à Mousson at Fumel, France. They are of 850mm external diameter, and vary in thickness from 85mm at the base, where they carry 3,000 tons working load, to 40mm at the top. Bushings acting as sleeves around the gerberette support pins were factory welded and machined out for accurate alignment. At column base a Kreutz spherical bearing transfers the load to the foundations, permitting rotation.

THE TENSION TIE typically consists of 7m lengths of solid round bar of 200mm diameter, threaded on either end. The top is screwed clockwise and the bottom counter-clockwise into a boss (a giant nut) at the tip of the gerberette.

THE GERBERETTE is a single cast piece made in Rohrbach by Heckel Blaihart, linking the tension tie, compression column, and truss girder. It weighs 9.6 tons and is 8.2m long overall. All points of contact between it and other pieces are machined, and need to move. The development and refinement of the gerberette form epitomises development of the other cast pieces. The central problem to be solved was how to link the truss girder, column, and tie without putting any eccentric load into the column. A column is very sensitive to eccentric load, and even a small eccentricity would have had a big effect on its size. Spherical bearings allow the gerberette to flex and rotate without transmitting moments, eccentric loads, to the column. The gerberette form, which follows closely the moment envelope, was developed in conjunction with the founders, and had a minimum wall thickness everywhere of 35mm to facilitate metal flow. The actual cast form contained headers and pouring points which brought the weight as cast up to 17 tons. The form of the openings, both around the column and the saddle (the support point on the column) derive from the erection sequence. The gerberette rode down the column at right angles to its final position, and turned into position at its final height.

THE TRUSS GIRDER has a continuous double-tube compression chord, each tube being 450mm in diameter and of varying thickness, and a continuous double solid round for the bottom tension chord. The latter are sized to carry the forces found at the different sections of the truss girder, and vary from 225mm diameter rounds in the center to two 160mm diameter rounds at the ends. These are fitted and welded into cast steel nodes, or coupling members, which lie between the double compression members or double tension members, and onto which are butt-welded the single diagonal struts, alternatively tube and rod, depending on forces carried. The truss girder has 2.5m effective depth, 2.85m depth overall, spans 44.8m between supports, and carries a load of 720 tons when fully loaded.

THE FLOORS act as horizontal beams, transmitting the horizontal forces from wind and stability to either end of the building, as well as carrying the vertical load between truss girders. The floor between any two truss girders consists of a series of 110mm concrete panels 6.4m x 10.8m, compositely connected to steel I-profiles 500mm deep which span onto truss girders, i.e. a distance of 12.8m. The panels are alternately pinned and continuous to enable the truss girders to deflect independently of the floor. By subdividing the floor into discrete panels, the compression in the top boom of the trussed girder, to which the floor is attached, is not transmitted into the floor. The compression shortening is up to 40mm over the full length of a truss girder, and requires a tolerance gap of 6mm between panels.

At either end of the building the truss girders are interconnected to form a BRACED-FRAME GABLE END. The braced effect is achieved by using the bending strength of the truss girders to produce a Vierendeel action in a vertical plane.

THE LONGITUDINAL CROSS-BRACING at the front piazza facade and the rear Rue du Renard facade consists of 60mm diagonal rods of high-tensile steel (E60), with threaded ends.

THE HORIZONTAL BRACING connects the floors to the outer longitudinal bracing and to the columns. It is used principally to stabilize the columns against buckling. To do this, the stability bracing occurs at every level and connects the columns to the floor. The full bracing occurs at alternate levels to coincide with the horizontal members of longitudinal

The southeast corner, with a movable maintenance gantry parked near the gerberettes. Transverse bracing on column planes inside the building would have obstructed the space, so all such bracing is concentrated on the north and south facades. The braces connect the truss girders, with the most sizeable at the bottom gerberette corners, making rigid the elements that are flexible elsewhere bracing. It is left out where vertical circulation is necessary.

Summary of steel frame erection progress:

(1) The first bay, the southernmost one, erected by 31 October 1974.

(2) By 29 November, the third bay was being erected.

(3) By 27 December, three bays were complete.

(4) By 24 January 1975, the fifth bay was under way.

(5) Superstructure was half complete (six and a half bays) by the end of February.

(6) 30 April 1975: main erection near finish, and bracing following quickly.

Fire safety had been a continuing preoccupation throughout the design of Beaubourg—so much so that for several years one of Renzo Piano's main jobs was representing the design team at fire safety consultations and negotiations. When steelwork was already being delivered, official reconsideration forced some crucial last-minute design changes.

The fire safety officials had decided in late 1971 that Beaubourg, a public building with many experimental aspects to its proposed structure, had to be watched and monitored carefully. Two working parties were set up. One, mainly scientific, was headed by Colonel Cabray of the safety commission CSTB; with this group, tests and trials were made on almost all of Beaubourg's safety equipment. The second working party, more administrative, was directed by M. Blot of the Préfecture of Paris police. With them the design team studied, and sometimes were allowed to modify, regulations relating to emergency exits and access by fire vehicles.

In late 1972, Piano and Bordaz settled some vital agreements with the authorities. The assumed capacity of the building above the ground floor would be 4,000 visitors plus 800 staff. The entire building would be protected by sprinklers, except in certain zones where there would be substitute protection. Flame barriers between floors would have a one-hour rating: they would be deemed adequate if they stopped flames for an hour (it had earlier been decided that the overall fire resistance of the primary structure should be two hours). The *charge calorifique*, or potential for combustion per square meter, would not exceed that of a certain amount of paper—established at 15 kilograms.

The effect of having to deal with CSTB, the police, the insurance authority SOCOTEC, and many other groups that sometimes were only marginally concerned with safety, started to produce, it was gloomily thought by the design team, a tower of umbrellas of protective rules. There were often three or four umbrellas, one above the other. Piano was tactful, but some rules seemed to defy logic. For instance, the design team was being called upon to protect beams too massive to need protection. In a fire, the problem with steel beams arises only above a critical temperature. The question of the steel actually getting that hot would depend on a relationship between the surface exposed to fire and the steel mass. For the cross-section in question, the relationship was extremely low because of small surface in relation to mass—with the conduction rate of steel, it would have taken well over two hours (the allowable minimum for this particular case) in a constant fire to build up to the critical temperature of 700 degrees Celsius determined for the alloy steel.

The proof of this was theoretical, but engineers could show with elementary calculations that it would be so. In early 1973, Colonel Cabray decided that no theoretical proofs would be considered by CSTB, only practical ones, and all Piano's impassioned pleas were rejected. The date was already very late since steelwork details had long since been determined, and fire protection coatings hadn't even been explored for many of the steel members reckoned to have sufficient mass for safety. The Arup research team in London had backed up the design team in work on materials (Turlogh O'Brien), foundations (David Henkel), structural design (John Blanchard), and general fire safety (Margaret Law). Now they had to look at enveloping the entire indoor primary structure in fire-resistant coatings.

As serious as this was, worse was to come. In September 1974, the biggest function-and-cost crisis over fire safety blew up when the

CSTB abruptly asked for a two-hour fire wall instead of a one-hour flame barrier along the Rue de Renard face, between the mechanical equipment and the interior. The CSTB justified this change of requirement by the fact that the mechanical equipment was going to be heavier than previously supposed and might endanger the structure if there was local collapse in a fire. Since the design logic of having mechanical equipment on the exterior depended partly on economies deriving from the assumed greater fire safety, this was bitter news. Perhaps the ductwork and other services should have been inside after all! Certainly two-hour protection on inside mechanical equipment was unheard of. But heavy transformers, water tanks, elevators, and elevator counterweights were the main worry, and for flexibility they would have been outside in any case, so the CSTB's decision was only untimely and hard to accept, not nonsensical. Rice believed that a certain destructive fire, much in the French news at that time, had forced the working party to rethink.

The implications were alarming because of time, appearances, and costs. The time delay was because of the new fire barrier wall. Its addition meant that most of the interiors had to be replanned. As for Beaubourg's looks, the transparency of what would have been wire glass facing the colorful ductwork was lost. The cost issue, bad enough, also affected fees, since the design team's own profit depended on meeting the agreed budget of November 1971. But Piano reluctantly acknowledged that the decision was prudent. Only about a third of the total fire safety precautions had the effect of extra tiers of umbrellas. The rest were needed. No one wanted to have designed a building where, for lack of intelligent foresight, people got hurt. One of the few advantages in the length of time it takes to plan and build is that most unwise decisions can be reconsidered, and errors can be rectified, in the drawn-out process.

TECHNICAL NOTES ON FIRE SAFETY[2]

The main objectives were to reduce the risk of fire, to ensure the safe evacuation of the public and the safe intervention of the fire brigade, to protect the main building structure for two hours, and to protect the building's contents.

Organizationally, the principal method for fire safety was to restrict public access to manageable numbers in case escape was necessary. Turnstiles at the main escalators were to count people going to upper floors, and those would be stopped at 3,500. Combustibility of contents would be no more than the equivalent of 10kg of wood per square meter except for the library. Almost all materials used on interiors would be incombustible (steel, aluminum, inert materials), or combustible with great difficulty (e.g., carpet fixed to incombustible decking with water-based adhesive).

Architecturally, the key fire measures were the positioning of columns and gerberettes outside, having all escape exits for public leading directly outside, having all escape stairs and other main vertical circulation outside, having all main mechanical and electrical equipment outside on public floors, and reducing to a minimum interior vertical ducting and services. Typical fire rating would be two hours within the building, and three hours between the building and the underground car park.

"Active" technical systems for surveillance and fire detection would include heat detectors and TV cameras, as well as pressure gauges on door controls, column pumps and sprinkler systems, all of which turn on lights at the fire detection display panel in the control center. Remote alarms and personnel notification would operate from the control center, with controls for fire dampers, fire doors, operation of smoke extracts and intake of fresh air, elevators (made to not stop on a floor where there is a fire), air conditioning, sprinkler pumps, inert gas and carbon dioxide extinguishing systems.

To protect superimposed layers of service networks in major corridors at lower levels from collapse, there was to be a fire-resistant steel structure suspended below. Escape routes for the public were to be cleared of smoke by suction through networks of fireproof ducts. The enormous volume of the Forum[3] was to be dealt with in a system of eight helicoidal smoke extract fans capable of operating for a long time at 200 degrees Celsius. Throughout, fresh air grilles, damped or opened from a fire detection board, were placed to prevent too large a depressurization during smoke extract. All fire control cabling was to be separately circuited and fireproofed.

---

2 This is an edited version of notes by Ove Arup and Partners.
3 See page 156.

"Passive" technical systems were the strategies used in the building fabric itself. The whole of the exposed external steelwork was to be protected from effects of internal fire by water filling, by fire screens in the facade, by selective redundancy which would allow certain members to be lost in a fire without affecting the stability of the building, and by sprinklers. Theoretical projection of flames from the facade was studied, and heat in steelwork elements calculated to ensure that none would reach critical temperature in a two-hour fire.

Internally, temperature of steel elements was to be limited to 450 degrees Celsius after a two-hour fire by using different tactics. Tubular truss girder members would be protected with about 19mm of Rocksil, a rockwool, with a stainless steel enclosing casing. Solid steel bottom truss members, with larger heat conductivity since they were solid, would use 6mm of Capoflex compressible ceramic fiber. Maranite asbestos cover was to be used where Rocksil would look too thick. All nodes and exposed floor beams were to be sprayed with Mandolite vermiculite cement, following the forms. On elements not visible, blown Vanifibre was to be used. Other floor beams were to be protected with Wannifibre. Tertiary steel,[4] interior and exterior walkways were to be protected by intumescent paint, which foams into an insulating layer on contact with fire, providing protection for a half hour. Mechanical equipment on the Rue de Renard facade was to be protected by facade panels: sandwiches of Pical insulation within stove enameled steel plate.

The most serious fire problems arise when interior equipment collapses during either public escape or fire brigade intervention. Heavier elements collapsing might even break through the floor slabs, which would jeopardize the fire containment measures. To combat this, interior elements were analyzed in "collapse stages," and designed accordingly. Non-protected elements, stable for ten minutes, included lights, aluminum cladding, lighting rails, awnings. Lightweight unprotected elements, stable for 30 minutes, included false ceiling panels and false floor elements. Ducts, pipes and main cable runs were to have deliberate breaking positions so that during their fall they would avoid collapsing part of the facade or creating too large a hole. Protected medium heavy elements, stable for 30 minutes, included mechanical equipment service beams, the Cinakothèque structure,[5] awning frames, ceilings of conference rooms and toilets. Protected heavy elements, stable for 45 minutes, included mezzanine structures. With intumescent paint, stability would be assured for 30 minutes; the remaining problem was to soften the impact

---

4 Tertiary steel is steelwork not part of the main building structure. A further explanation follows on pages 144–145.
5 See page 162.

Part of the east elevation. A late official ruling that dictated a two-hour fire barrier between the occupied building spaces and the mechanical equipment meant that latticelike views of the interior from the east side were lost

on the floor. A cable, protected and non-active for the first half hour of a fire, would stop the fall of mezzanines about one meter above the floor, before losing strength due to high temperature, and slowly lowering the load the rest of the way.

• • • • • •

After the early days, the design team divisions didn't work together much. Alan Stanton's "systems" team, working on toilets, telephones, and other internal and external systems, found they could work separately from the superstructure and facade teams because, once a definition of the service pattern of the building had been established, as well as the limitations that the building would impose in spaces and routes, and the places where heavy loads or conduits could be put and places where they couldn't be, it was no longer vital to work closely. Compared to other large modern architectural projects, Beaubourg relied more on the initiative of team captains. This was as Piano and Rogers expected.

In the circumstances of high speed and a relative freedom of maneuver, teams sometimes worked more closely with their industrial supporters than with their designer colleagues. In Eric Holt's team for the development of the facade, the facade contractors CFEM played a central role. At one stage CFEM had seven designers of its own in the team office. Since attachable-detachable flexibility was a key objective, matters of fire safety, structural steel protection, movement, insulation, solar screening, and all other ordinary facade issues could be taken up and solved individually, if that contributed (or perhaps only alluded) to flexibility. Thus, even exterior skin, solved on most modern buildings with some form of integrated cladding, was developed at Beaubourg as an explicit dissection, its wind bracing separate from the wall panels and its solar control separate from the glass, like an illustrator's "exploded view" of construction that somehow actually got built that way. Beaubourg's team of autonomous but integrated designers and manufacturers helped to achieve a special liberated aesthetic.

In the design nomenclature, the primary steel was the basic structure, assumed to be capable of remaining in place for centuries without

View from the museum terrace, fourth level, facing west. As part of a many-sided approach to fire safety, the hollow centrifugally cast main columns were designed to be filled with circulating water to maintain the steel at a sufficiently low temperature in a fire (this concept was made possible by the crystalline structure of cast steel, which tends to hold rust in place, forming a protective skin). Flexible architectural planning allows the pedestrian gallery, separated from the terrace by a gap at the line of columns, to remain open when the museum is closed

needing replacement or modification. The secondary steel included the floor elements. Tertiary steel included all the extensible, modifiable, possibly provisional, pieces. Their actual purpose was to support galleries, external escalators, external elevators, ductwork. Other tertiary steel parts were designed to support external audiovisual screens still unbuilt. Tertiary steel components followed a simple design vocabulary of bars, eyes, pins, and variable angles so that most conceivable external building changes could adapt the same components, or use the same vocabulary.

Peter Rice and Laurie Abbott were jointly responsible for the function and form of the tertiary steel. This task had special problems, because tertiary steel was the link between all the other main elements. As it was meant to be a flexible system, some of the fabricators could not be told until the last moment exactly what their steelwork would be supporting. The organization and detailed development of the steelwork required close cooperation between contractors and design team on the one hand, and still more contractors on the other.

The work process in Abbott's team's main effort, "superstructure and mechanical services," was representative of how all the Beaubourg teams worked. Though Abbott himself had never completed his formal architectural training, he had a true grasp of complexities, and his graphic skills were so highly developed that he could sketch three-dimensional views of theoretical air conditioning duct configurations while the builder waited. Abbott was a blunt fellow and was generally kept away from clients. Five Japanese architects made up his team, partly through earlier friendships, and Abbott found a dependable cultural resource in their pragmatic Japanese training and attitude. He would explain that they could draw, make models, and supervise construction all day, without asking Abbott and each other a lot of soul-searching and time-wasting aesthetic or polemical questions.

In dealing with electricity, water, heating, ventilating, and air conditioning on the exterior, Abbott organized things with Tom Barker, the Arup chief mechanical equipment engineer. Architects' knowledge of mechanical equipment is generally limited, but mechanical engineers usually aren't expected to explain beyond single-line drawings of what connects to what. The industry gets both architect and engineer through the job. At Beaubourg, performance requirements were severe, and the public was intended to actually view the result. Things had to be done differently. Anticipating that mechanical equipment would take a third of the total budget and a quarter of the total space of a highly serviced building like Beaubourg, Abbott discussed with Barker the building's requirements: the divisions of space, the necessary maximums and minimums. Barker responded loosely, so they could start to understand simply what orders of magnitude would be involved, for example, in Beaubourg's air conditioning system.

Abbott's team first studied air cooling and ventilation because air handling equipment was the largest mechanical service. Soon they were dealing in detail with plumbing services, electrical services, fire sprinkler services, fire detection services. Ultimately, to avoid interfering conflicts, they all had to be studied in parallel.

After meetings, the architects would do sketches and rough axonometrics (three-dimensional drawings with all planes in scale), to illustrate what they thought was meant. They would next present them to the interprofessional—and quite soon, interconstructional—group for checking and agreement. Cabinet Trouvin, an Arup mechanical equipment consultant that helped in the early stages to prepare tenders, advised Tom Barker here too. The architects' sketches would be revised, and sometimes rough models were made. Not until they felt confident did Abbott's team start to do orthographic (flat plane) drawings, and then they were still explorative. In the course of Beaubourg's design, the team did perhaps five complete revisions of such drawings. Their main purpose wasn't for construction, but checking: for the mechanical engineers and suppliers to understand what they were doing, and for the architects to keep watch on how things were going. The orthographic drawings were almost a postmortem.

Since mechanical service elements were to be prefabricated, they progressed like the earlier example of the mechanical ventilator control. What was wanted was, first, a specification of the element,

Pedestrian gallery on the west elevation. The necessary working components are unconcealed and subject to replacement without undue practical or aesthetic problems. Hung below the cantilever gerberettes are rails for traveling maintenance cabs. The glass curtain wall to the right is held by light mullions with trussed outrigger elements for stiffness. Semiautomatic rolling shutters shade the glass. The horizontal cylindrical member connecting the tips of the gerberettes to the left is a tension tie 200mm (8in) in diameter, occurring on alternate floors

with diagrams where necessary. The specification would elicit the supplier's own particular design, taking into account his or her own experience and usage; the supplier would produce shop drawings showing precisely what was about to be supplied. The shop drawings would be checked by the design team to make sure that they agreed with the spec and that the design was satisfactory in all other unspecified particulars. The element then arrived already made up. All that was really needed then from the design team was a coordination drawing. This had to show the location, fixing, and connection for every element. It could be (and usually was) diagrammatic, not pictorial.

When they got to the fabrication stage, the fabrication teams of most of the supplying companies came to work in the Beaubourg design office. The coordination party was Barker, Abbott, and the Japanese team, plus representatives from Otis, from four air conditioning suppliers, from two electrical suppliers, two plumbing suppliers, the cooling tower people, the glazing people, and the steel people. The overall building picture was not of interest to most of the people in this crowd. All the contractors wanted to know about was their own pipe, duct, or shaft. Could it go into the building? Would it fit? What did it connect to?

Though clearly someone had to be satisfied that it would not only connect but also look all right, and that was part of Abbott's primary responsibility too, Abbott maintained that this was done not from any overall picture or precalculation but from knowledge of need and experience of the building. He felt what was needed; he flew the work by the seat of his pants. It was a good example of "termite creativity," a phrase once used by the film theorist Manny Farber to describe what happens (as may happen in any design endeavor) when one simply decides to pay attention to nothing but what one understands from within.

Beaubourg's mechanical equipment was exposed to view partly for fire safety, partly to keep the building's interiors free and flexible, partly for expression, and partly through the design recognition that it was the major building element likely to be soonest replaced, upgraded, adapted, or made more energy-efficient. The history of other long-life buildings showed this. Putting the mechanical equipment mostly outside the building was not so good as far as weather resistance was concerned, however. The guts of the building were out in the weather.

Electrical gear had to be safe against regular dousing. Water supplies and drainage had to resist freezing. Sheet metal air handling ducts had to be finished to resist rust. Fire shutters had to shut, when they were called to do so. Elevator rails and elevator safety devices had to work every time—and so on. Solving a few major problems created others.

In working through the ways to achieve weather resistance, Abbott's team discovered that a lot of solutions were ready-made: electrical gear was already manufactured to suit outside conditions, and plumbing practice already had standard details of expansion loops and so on that suit extreme temperature changes. All exterior pipes and air ducts would have to be jacketed in insulation, but good practice would have demanded the same indoors. The crucial matter proved to be finish. Finishes needed to be really special, and more costly than if the mechanical equipment had been entirely within. Both Abbott's and Holt's teams devoted a lot of time to researching the best and longest-lasting finishes for structure, equipment, and facades, as John Young did again later with his slightly different program requirements on furniture. Various answers seemed attractive, some of which—such as an American subliming paint (which gives off a protective gas in a fire) called Thermolag, an aerospace spin-off—never materialized, because of communication problems with the companies, or experimental technology that was not yet dependable. Capital cost versus running cost was a constant issue. In the end different finishes were used for different requirements.

All finishes had to stand up for a long time, no matter what their other purposes. For instance, the exterior air ducts, first jacketed in insulation, were then enclosed in an outer casing of aluminum (only the covering was aluminum; the ducts themselves were designed in galvanized steel). For these, an electrostatically applied colored powder was put on in the factory and then baked (or "stoved") to make it melt. It was reasoned that when the factory finishes applied there and elsewhere were breaking down after their ten-year life or whatever, the elements would have to be refinished in place. But the ductwork wouldn't be likely to be in use much longer than ten years, because air handling equipment in complex buildings is constantly subject to alteration and replacement.

The electrical design problems were maddening. For safety considerations and with economies of scale, all the energy used at Beaubourg was to be electric, and consequently, the distribution and control of electricity formed a potentially important part of the visual understanding of the building. But the physical realization of an electrician's work is unimportant: it lacks scale, drama, even any need for exact location. To electrical contractors, as long as the power supply, ratio phasing, fusing, trip switches, and so on create a workable and safe system, the looks and locations of the actual cables and control boxes are only a very small part of their job, and the last to interest them.

The easiest work method for an electrician is not to be given an exact design or to be asked for one but to be handed a floor plan and then to manage to turn up shortly before the job's finish with a vanful of wire in order just to wire up what is there. For the design team, this was frustrating. Most of the building elements had been decided, and some had even been installed, before the electrical contractor had settled on a coherent response. An electrician's method was more blind than their own termite creativity at its most extreme.

It took a lot of aggravation to get electrical information, with neither side having much sense of what was desired. Ultimately, although transformers and cable connections were beautifully made, their size and arrangement was never fully planned by the design team, and some of the locations of cableways happened almost by chance.

The matter of the building's colors was one of the few issues where Robert Bordaz was somewhat out of accord with the design team. On the architects' side, Rogers, Abbott, and Stanton were mainly involved. Rogers had always favored bright primary and secondary colors as a way to "humanize" hard technological components. Abbott was concerned mostly from a technical point of view since he was investigating the durability of finishes. Stanton and others supported the idea of color coding: he thought each system should have its bright color. There were no disagreements within the team—all wanted "happy colors," as they called them. Prior to construction, a large model at 1:50 scale was being made of the final design, and the model maker asked for colors. That was when the battle started.

It seems a deep psychological truth that every interested party in any circumstances of choosing color becomes a color expert. The client hired a *couleuriste* as advisor, but being an excellent *couleuriste,* he had simply said to the architects, You adopt the color philosophy you want—I realize that my job is to defend the color choices. Abbott, Franchini, Rogers, and Stanton visited the model maker, bringing color samples such as chips of plastic cups from the Rogerses' flat, snips from magazines, the bottom of someone's tie. They asked the model maker to use the standard coded system, but where normal maintenance engineering color codes were lacking, they advised him that the structure should be in chrome yellow, the hot air ducts red, the cold air ducts blue. They departed. The model arrived a few weeks later in entirely different colors. In the interim, parties from the Établissement Public had sneaked down to the model maker and had substituted a new array.

The model as the client would have it was equipped with a structure that was brown ("the color of a match-striking surface"), and everything else was blue. St. Laurent might love this, the architects indignantly thought, but it seemed to them fatuously voguish and too dateable for a building. Fortunately, the Établissement Public seemed to have reservations as soon as the model was unveiled, and they put a notice on it saying *"COULEURS PROVISIONNELLES,"* of which Stanton prudently took a photo for possible evidence. An altercation began that was unparalleled since the early days of client-design team fee bargaining and mutual distrust. Perhaps we aren't right, said the client representatives, but the architects aren't right either. Bordaz attempted to be mediator, but word was leaking out to the press. He decided to overtly consult Pontus Hulten, the head of the museum of modern art (who in fact had originally suggested brown). After all, Bordaz thought, Hulten was qualified to talk about this. He also had more political prestige to deploy at that moment than the architects and might be able to overrule them, as he had already started doing on the furniture and interior colors in the museum spaces.

With the matter openly referred to him, Hulten said that if brown wasn't it, there was only one color for the structure, and that was blue, and the only blue was the deep blue of French workmen's overalls. It transpired that this was a Prussian blue so dark as to obscure all details in most lighting conditions. The architects argued that it would be like painting the structure black. As an experiment, some of Hulten's color was applied to a cardboard drawing tube just to see what a cylindrical form of that color would look like. When the trial tube was set up at the end of the studio, all visible shading vanished and it looked like a flat stripe. Hulten agreed that overalls blue didn't work. Then they started talking about silver, light browns, possibly grays. Hulten was living opposite the Eiffel Tower, and they talked about that; the Eiffel Tower was once multicolored like a rainbow from top to bottom. Now it is a light khaki. Hulten admired the way the khaki tower reflected sky colors depending on the time of day and the light. Then Hulten backtracked to silver. But silver was an impractical choice since matching finishes would be difficult, and it was no good for economical maintenance (the vastly more expensive stainless steel silvery casing that Richard Rogers was to provide around Lloyd's of London's building elements was still years in the future). So the preferences proliferated, and no one seemed to be able to agree on anything. But Stanton, with Abbott's support and Rogers's agreement, kept coming back to a standard code of colors, and that idea eventually outlasted the rest.

When the standard code of colors was adopted, the usual maintenance-engineer color convention had to be added to, and this was done slightly differently than had at first been suggested to the model maker. All air conditioning ducts, for which there wasn't a conventional color, were made blue. Red was relegated to the movement systems. Water was to be green, and electrical systems yellow. The color for the structure itself remained to be settled. Someone proposed light gray, because since

The scheme of coded colors in full array on the service-side east elevation includes white for structure (plus the largest ventilation components, as decreed by Mme. Pompidou), silver gray for stairs and elevator structure, blue for ventilation, green for plumbing and fire control piping, red for elevator motor rooms and shafts, yellow-orange for electrical elements. The choice of colors involved more heated discussion than most matters structure was both inside and outside the building, it had to be fairly neutral—it also needed to show shade so the modeling and detail of the forms could be seen. Rogers said, Let's make it white and have done with it. It was finally agreed by all that white would be fine with the stainless steel fire insulation jacketing on the truss girders. Off-white, plus the coded colors, was ultimately carried out. Just before erection and completion, the cooling towers on the roof and the biggest air intakes on the ground were painted white over the blue-coded plastic coatings, by order of Madame Pompidou via the president.

Some outside architects, members of the press, and a few participants in the client group were sensitive to the non-Frenchness of the design team, and especially to its Anglo-Saxon component. It was obvious to the design team that Beaubourg without French work would have been impossible. Yet the sensitivity had to be recognized. The French architectural profession as a whole had accepted the international competition with a dignified lack of chauvinism. (In the view of some entrants at the time, France was the only nation in the world with the cultural maturity to allow an international competition to be countenanced for such an important project.) However, the actual design of the winning entry proved too much for a faction of French architects. One phrase in particular in the jury report had infuriated them, because it seemed to sum up what they found grievously lacking in the Piano & Rogers design. The words appeared in the criticism of some other schemes. The jury had averred that "freedom cannot be merely formal; that a 'monument' is vain that would have no other function besides expressing an architectural 'gesture'; . . . and that 'art for art's sake' can be the contrary of art." Directed toward a profession handicapped (as Piano saw it) by the École des Beaux-Arts's teaching that creativity in architecture was principally a matter of self-expression, it was hardly surprising that this faction seized on the French word for "gesture" and, forming an ad hoc organization called *Geste Architecturale,* flew into the attack. They raised money and brought lawsuits to stop the work.

There were seven lawsuits during Beaubourg's progress. Mostly they were nuisance allegations, though one, a case against Prouvé as architect-chairman of the jury (it was alleged that the jury was invalid because Prouvé had never received a diploma), gratuitously offended the great man. Another suit, a quibble over the site boundary, actually stopped building work for 15 days: it was based on the fact that deeds showed a historic mistake over boundaries on the south side between the Ville de Paris and national ownership, which were both parties to the land transaction in any case. Realizing that any delay attracted antagonists seeking to end the job permanently, Bordaz coolly kept on a skeleton force until a court order allowed work to continue. However, it was a very serious matter.

Though all the suits were eventually disposed of, they were part of a growing and disheartening fusillade of criticism in press, political offices, and public factions that had arisen (of which chauvinism was only one aspect) and that went on savaging the scheme. One petition that the architects were shown was from 60 academicians and intellectuals objecting to the construction of such a monstrosity. It was highly believable; yet actually, it proved to be a rather telling joke: the objections had been raised not against Beaubourg, but in 1888 against the Eiffel Tower.

An outcome of all the attacks was that the architects learned to stop being self-effacing and began to suggest more vigorously how their own ideas should be understood, even if the client might not have necessarily concurred. "It will be a cultural supermarket, won't it?" a journalist asked Rogers. "I have no objection to 'supermarket,' my objection is to the word 'cultural,'" he replied. This remark was widely quoted and deplored in the usual antagonistic circles. But over all the criticism from without and the resentments from within, Bordaz never gave up or got tired. He remained fresh and competent, controlling everything.

7   Toward opening night

While construction proceeded at a great rate, considerable design issues remained. The planning of activities changed constantly, virtually until the opening. The allocation of space had originally been planned around the position of the library, partly because the museum lacked effective representation until Hulten became its head; the library client had insisted on a three-level library, and thus everything, including the museum, fitted around it. Later the library client began to accept the idea of a one-or two-level library, which would have meant more freedom to plan, but it was then too late for such a major switch. The key idea that stayed was the "activity sandwich," with the most popular activities destined for street level and at the top. The public would pass more specialized levels between, and they might be lured in. A new feature, the open multi-use space on the ground floor (now known as the Forum), was suggested by the architects. They intended it to have multiple uses at the same time: music, film, talks, exhibitions. The client accepted it, but thought the space could also be used for an indoor garden or permanent exhibit.

There was a late, largely illusory fear that the building's volume would be insufficient. The definitive design had reverted to a skeletal

The "Forum" space on the ground floor. The overhead catwalks and channels were provided below the main structure for lighting and the rigging of temporary displays

framework similar to that shown by the competition design, but the framework was filling up, which the design team didn't like. Since there were seven meters between floors, a way to keep some of the structure empty was to put in intermediate levels where lower ceilings wouldn't hurt. The design team looked at many ways to do that: galleries down both sides; all sorts of cross-sectional variations. They eventually settled on the idea of a floor assembly that could be hung in any bay from I-girders alongside the trusses. This device became known as the mezzanine.

The primary steel structure had been made strong enough to take the superimposition of two mezzanine units, about 6 meters by 10 meters each, in every bay. These could be stacked at one end and rolled out as needed, with the I-girders functioning as hanging tracks. A slice of the budget was set aside for 33 mezzanine units—at first to be Rolls-Royces of mechanical sophistication, each with its own traction motor, lighting, and air conditioning that could be plugged in above. This was over-luxurious. It was trimmed down to a simpler, lighter mezzanine that could be moved by attaching a separate motor or by hand-winching. Finally, a detailed analysis of the fire requirements revealed that the units couldn't safely be made to roll at all, but had to be unbolted, jacked down, and put up again. While these developments were happening the rest of the building was developing too, and the mezzanine budget was eroding. Alan Stanton, the team leader, watched with alarm as the final primary steel costs were slightly high, the facade costs came in over the top, the tertiary steel was too much. All were gnawing at his little mezzanine budget, which was being left for last. He argued for the mezzanines, but the client by then had become unconvinced about them. As the users came to be faced with actually planning the occupancy of the vast spaces they were given, their demand for extra space was dwindling. What were the mezzanines really for? Why should they be there? Who needed them? The only user who remained very interested was the librarian: all libraries have mezzanines, and he thought he wanted at least one. Pontus Hulten was willing to consider them. He asked for a mock-up at the old museum at the Palais. In the end, only a single mezzanine unit was provided at Beaubourg, more or less as a sample. It was set in the museum in an inconspicuous place. It doesn't move. The remains of the mezzanine budget were used toward the potentiality for future mezzanines: providing rails in the exhibition spaces, and supplying bolt fixing points elsewhere. (In 1979 the client was asking for mezzanines again.)

Even when in receipt of a client's greatest good will and confidence, an architect's creative scope beyond the given design brief is naturally limited. At Beaubourg, the architects had control only over what they were instructed to do, not over anything at all they felt like proposing. Only through successive discussions and persistence did they manage to get to design the lighting, the interior partitions, and eventually the furniture. Piano & Rogers was consulted about the graphics—the contract for signs was awarded on the basis of an international graphics competition—but the architects were going to be left off the assessment jury for that, until they protested.

Work in the P & R London office was running down, so toward the end of the Beaubourg job, John Young began to go to Paris every other week. Some specific help was needed in furniture design. Piano and Rogers had gotten worried that the whole logic of the building, with its principle of construction and materials, was getting lost when applied to the furniture. Young was expected to help imbue the furniture with the right design stuff. Within the vast spaces of Beaubourg, and especially in administrative areas, the furniture would become crucial, because there would be almost no partitions, hangings, or other subdivisive tricks to define space. As someone said, if it was crappy furniture, they were going to get crappy interiors. So the first step to be taken was polemical. Furniture was termed "internal systems" by the architects, to be considered as another construction within the fabric of the building, controlled by the same constraints of module, fire, weight, color, and so on.

With signs of reluctance, Bordaz allowed Young, with his team including Gianni Franchini and Jean Huc, to change the client's designs, keeping within the limits of the previous low prices. The first new decision was to define and design flexible components that would deal adequately with every furniture problem—not for chairs, desks, and tables alone, but for all the special museum display equipment, sales counters, and mobile book stalls. The biggest furniture company in France, Strafor, had already gotten the bookshelf units, counters, display units, and cloakroom equipment to provide four of the nine furniture packages, which helped standardization. Young steered them into adopting the same joints and attachments across the board. The fire safety constraint meant a categorical denial of any combustible material, and everything had to have what was called an "M zero" rating— incombustible, and having no surface spread of flame. In some ways this made things easier for Piano & Rogers's nuts-and-bolts mentality as already expressed in the building. The architects naturally favored metal furniture, and it was a relief to be able to rule out wood for safety reasons. The question came down to whether the metal should be steel or aluminum. Steel won out because it was cheaper, stronger, and lighter looking.

With steel, the finish was crucial. It was decided that it would be a stoved acrylic finish. Young worried about this, but later he was sure it was the correct decision. Everything concerning materials had to be brought before the CSTB, the insurance approving authority. (It was resident in the office at this stage. If you wanted to use a new material, it wasn't necessary to write a letter, only to go up a flight of stairs where you would get the answer in a few minutes.) The CSTB recommended stoved acrylic rather than a stoved epoxy finish. Acrylic isn't as hard and scratches more easily than epoxy, but it has the advantage of not chipping in big flakes like an old enameled saucepan.

The bright green color of the furniture derived from the simple color-code attitude. Blues, reds, and white had already been used on main elements. Wire mesh and semiconstructional parts of furniture would be in silvery zinc. The only part of the Beaubourg interiors where these colors weren't used was in the museum, where Pontus Hulten demanded white for his furniture as well as for his mechanical equipment and everything else but the paintings.

Hulten and the architects had many disagreements, though his attitude was understood if not entirely appreciated. He had to make many deals and compromises with benefactors and their estates simply to have been able to bring most of the art collection intact to Beaubourg. The most

The piazza and west elevation, with the "wavy line" of escalators admired by juror Philip Johnson

serious matters concerned the museum director's attitude toward the spaces themselves: the exposed mechanical equipment, and the height. It was decided that all the service ducts and conduits would be white in the museum to reduce competition with artworks. If necessary, ceiling "flats" could be dropped to create more intimate or special spaces. Beaubourg's great volumes could function like a sound stage around film sets, if that was called for.

In the museum, artificial light, daylight, and sunlight were to be regulated by mostly nonautomatic controls. One space-saving invention devised to order by the design team was *le Cinakothèque*. This was an overhead motorized rack of screens to allow curators or students the opportunity for viewing pictures not regularly on display, complete with outrigger lights. The screens were to hold paintings on both sides, stacking closely together like flats under a stage gridiron, each screen rising or falling at the push of a button.

In the library, bookstacks and reading areas were not to be kept separate, but mixed together—unlike most large libraries. The idea was to maintain open views through the bookcases and a flexible furniture arrangement to allow easy supervision and great adaptability. For expansion, there was the future possibility of mezzanines.

The piazza became merely the space left over on the site, for lack of agreement, sufficient funds, and specific instructions. This wasn't what the architects had hoped for or had originally proposed. Rogers and Stanton had looked at Times Square and Tivoli Gardens and had collected photos and data on every other urban public place they could think of. They tried hard to promote with the client the "nonprogrammed" activities: a children's area, live performances, outdoor movies, relaxing areas, play areas. They considered ice skating in the winter, a wading pool in the summer. But no money had been set aside for nonprogrammed activities. A replica of Brancusi's studio was to be built on the piazza, a concession to his estate that was deemed necessary in order not to lose the Brancusi sculpture collection. This was the only budgeted item.

Stanton was the team leader who bore the brunt of the lost mezzanines and the nonfinance for the piazza, but for him the final disaster and saddest loss was the deletion of the Oscar Nitzchke–like information screen on the facade. Technical control systems such as security, surveillance, public address, temperature monitoring, fire alarm, and so on were basic architectural responsibilities. In addition, an audiovisual department was set up within Beaubourg with the aid of ORTF, the French broadcasting system. But the outside information system had been an even more fundamental design proposition. The competition team had originally conceived of fast information delivered to motorists from the Rue de Renard facade, and more elaborate, complex, slower displays to be generated for pedestrians on the piazza and south-facing facades. But the proposed system was subject to the same sort of budget nibbling that the mezzanines suffered, and also, to an undoubted disinclination of the client to take much interest in any unstructured activities.

The design team had concentrated on bringing to realization the most practical element for exterior display: some sort of bright, rectangular screen on the piazza facade. Stanton researched all the Olympic-style scoreboard systems and light-emitting systems requiring a matrix of light bulbs coordinated by computer that could transmit a message. With enough bulbs, visual resolution could be quite high. With three colored bulbs for each dot, there could be a full-color high-resolution picture. But by then it would have cost billions of francs, and bulbs would have had to be changed regularly too. Rather than a lit board, a projection system was more practical, at least from the economic point of view.

The key problem for a projection system was interference of daylight. A very "high gain" screen was needed so that a lot of light would be reflected back, to overcome ambient sky light or even direct sunlight. Stanton heard that the client didn't seem convinced about a projection screen either. All this building already—why have more headaches? But Hulten became enthusiastic about the idea of illuminated posters and "supergraphics." An American called Billy Kluver had done experiments with lenticular screens—screens made with tiny mirrors. It was an old but undeveloped German invention whose time had seemingly come. Kluver and Stanton designed a lenticular screen to have 1,300,000 mirrors about two centimeters by one centimeter, of nickel coated with rhodium, and to be made by a specialist supplier near San Diego, California. Each mirror was to be slightly concave. Perfect alignment was necessary, and a special washing system was devised to sweep across and clean them all every day.

Rice and Stanton next designed a structure that was a huge arm like a horizontal oil derrick with the projector at the end. Nothing was to be on the piazza at all. The arm was to be bolted to the ends of the gerberettes, and the projectionist was to reach it by a catwalk. Light from the projector would be reflected from the lenticular screen, with little loss of brightness, to a specific area on the piazza large enough for 200 to 300 people, though looking at the screen from elsewhere it would show nothing. An array of pavement loudspeakers was to broadcast the sound in that area only. With a super high-power projector and a retractable cowl for shading the mirror lenses, the screen still would have to be kept to only about seven meters by ten meters for good light intensity, and at the scale of the building that seemed too small. Yet when the designers imagined a daytime, brightly lit moving picture in color, which was a high-fidelity image (not a coarse screen of dots), the impact was obviously going to be very considerable.

The exterior projection system was budgeted for 6,000,000 francs. It was finally priced way over that. The Établissement Public decided to drop it just a few months before opening, though not without internal protests: "Piccadilly Circus is lost on the French," complained Lombard, when it was too late. Some thought the real objection was the political fear of effective public address in the piazza. (In the old days revolutions had started in the Palais-Royal, another central open space.) Others defended the decision, saying the screen wasn't sufficiently thought through. To show pictures of crowd scenes on the screen taken with a roving camera wouldn't have cost much, but to make the display worthwhile would have cost a lot. If an exterior audiovisual presentation advertising, say, the new Fauve show needed to cost as much as the exhibition itself, they argued, it was better to spend the money on exhibitions rather than audiovisuals. Stanton's team's drawings and specifications were added to the pile of Beaubourg elaborations that might come about later.

After Giscard's radical budget cut, IRCAM was completely redesigned by the Piano & Rogers team of Mike Davies with Nori Okabe, Kenn Ruppard, and Jan Sircus; the Arup structural team; and Peutz & Associates, acoustic consultants. Pierre Boulez was actively engaged as client, and he had focused what had been in earlier stages a much less directed brief.

"The hole awaits the design," someone said. This had been the position when the work was stopped. The revised design fitted the hole but maintained the original premise at lower cost: an underground complex of studios and laboratories with very high performance requirements for music and acoustic research and synthesis. Taking up the theme of Beaubourg, it extended flexibility for critical acoustic zones in a number of different ways:

• Flexibility through variety: there was a range of nine sound studios.

• Flexibility by variability: interchangeable panels in all studios could alter reverberation times and other acoustic qualities. Standard panels were to be kept in a common pool.

• Flexibility via a special machine—the projection space: a studio of 4,000 cubic meters was continuously variable in volume and acoustic qualities by electronic means.

• Flexibility by extra kits: there was one demountable studio of standard elements, with others possible to add.

• Flexibility by structure and infill: non-load-bearing heavy partitions between load-bearing columns could be moved, altering studio or laboratory spaces.

• Flexibility by electronic means: an audio and computer and TV network linked all research, sound production, listening, and recording spaces.

IRCAM's redesign was thought by all participants to have been a clarification as well as a simplification. The most strikingly successful of Beaubourg's divisions, it was completed about 18 months after the rest.

. . . . . .

Four years had gone by under the greatest nervousness and operational pressures. As for staff spirit, just as morale was terrible in the first year or two, it began to sink again during the last year when the building was substantially designed and the design staff was shrinking. Morale described a bell curve over the course of the job. At the end, everyone was wondering about the future. Renzo Piano and Richard Rogers themselves were disagreeing on lots of things—but on methods of working, rather than on the building. They would unite at once if any outsider misunderstood the nature of the irritations.

As in any complex construction work, the trick for determining a completion date was to identify the "critical path" from among all the construction operations. The critical path is so called because it is the longest necessary sequence of operations of which none can be overlapped or eliminated. Once the critical path is identified (which is sometimes quite difficult in practice), other sequences of jobs can slip backward a bit, provided they don't thereby become part of the critical path themselves and lengthen it still further. On Beaubourg, the critical path had been the sequence involving the design, fabrication, and erection of the primary steel. In view of the difficulties there had been in deciding on a primary steel contractor and in meeting metallurgical specifications, the client at last accepted the reality of an extended critical path and agreed to have a revised completion date of December 1976.

Toward the end, it was also apparent that, because of accumulating irritations that seemed only natural under the circumstances, the operational communications between the design team, the management contractor, and other contractors had considerably deteriorated. Despite the extension of time, there was danger that the revised completion date

The covered, underground IRCAM (*Institut de Recherche et de Coordination Acoustique/Musique*), seen from Beaubourg. In August 1974, after Pompidou's death, the music and acoustic research center's budget was slashed by about a third and the design had to be scaled down. In this view, to the right of IRCAM's ground-level skylights and ventilation ducts, is a later addition by Renzo Piano of renovated existing buildings for extra offices, with a new tower for vertical circulation (under construction in 1989)

wouldn't be met unless steps were taken to restore good relations and a mutual sense of purpose. In September 1975 it was therefore agreed that GTM would draw up a new construction program for all outstanding work, indicating the order of priority for each section of the building in relation to the completion date. At the same time, the project-planning group at Arup would do a study on the design team itself, and make recommendations.

In some ways this slightly Orwellian notion proved helpful. "The team had got into a pattern of falling in love with the problems, and not producing solutions," one engineer said. As the Arup planning group supported the design team's approach and showed that the building would be completed on time, it gave confidence to the client and management contractor. The study was finished at the end of 1975. During the next few months, regular progress checks were carried out to reveal any items not in line with the program. Installation of furniture and equipment made for some disruption. The setting-up of exhibition displays and other intense preparations for opening Beaubourg meant that the last building work had to be organized on a day-to-day basis.

The revitalization of administrative efficiency surrounding the completion of programs was like the final burst of energy at the end of a runner's exhausting race. The process that created Beaubourg was already complete for many design team members; others, as well as looking forward to their own futures, were starting to look back.

In a group of 26 or so architects, there had been 11 nationalities. They had designed "every single bolt," as one put it—they produced 20,000 to 25,000 drawings. Though it had been decreed in April 1974 that the building would be known as the Centre Nationale d'Art et de Culture Georges Pompidou, to the team who had worked on it and to a large section of the public, especially in France, it would always be called Beaubourg.

They remembered the crises. Radical developments that threatened or actually caused disruption in the design and building process had been the fees and contract problems; the split of fees between Arup and P & R; changes of brief such as the addition of a fourth major department, IRCAM; the imposition of the budget in January 1972; height limit restrictions; unexpected fire-safety severity; the steel bid crisis; the steel specification misunderstanding; legal actions that led to the closing of the site in July 1974; the banks and the professional liability insurance; the lateness in appointing a new museum curator, who had ideas of his own; the death of Pompidou in 1974 with the calling-in of and amendments to the scheme by Giscard d'Estaing; and the problem of allocating responsibility for furnishings and interior design.

In retrospect, it was evident to the design team that a further six months could have been allowed for developing the design before construction work started, without affecting the eventual completion date of Beaubourg. Less fast-track construction would have been of great value to the design team in the early days, and would probably have benefited the project as a whole.

Beaubourg was finished within the revised timetable, within 3 percent of the outline program floor area, and within the 12 percent contingency margin of the budget. In summary, the figures were as follows (prepared May 1979; values in French francs of January 1973; at the time, one U.S. dollar was worth about 5.13 francs and one U.K. pound sterling was worth about 12 francs):

1	CONTRACTUAL COST ESTIMATE		325,770,000
2	COST OF WORK		
	Initial contracts	322,310,973	
	Variation orders contracted	85,958,666	
	Variation orders due (waterproofing)	13,718 approx.	
		———————	
	Final account (construction total)	408,283,359	
	Add: management contract	4,184,375	

Subtract:

a. program changes	23,529,388	
b. new security requirements	25,079,655	
3 COST OF WORK COMPARED TO ESTIMATE		363,858,691
Excess of 11.70%		38,088,691

Using the allowed 12 percent contingency margin to improve the building was, of course, deliberate, and part of the artistry of the financial management.

No fee penalty was imposed, though some of Arup's fee claims remained unresolved for years. As far as the building budget was concerned, the overall cost control was admirably tight, but Lennart Grut and Gerry Clarke of the Paris Arup office believed that the proportional expenditures could have been more tightly monitored. This might have happened if the quantity surveyors had been given the scope they normally had. The highest objective was not only to come in on total budget but to have everything weighted correctly— then one could be sure that valuable objectives in one program weren't sacrificed to cut costs in another program. At the end of the Beaubourg job the structure and the mechanical equipment took up 80 percent of the money, with 20 percent left for the rest. That wasn't clear enough to the architects in the course of the work, nor very satisfactory to them when they at last understood it.

The official opening was January 31, 1977. In the last days, hundreds of extra workmen were added. Almost the entire piazza was paved with cobbles in the 48 hours before the opening. Thousands of guests were invited from all over the world—the Paris galleries, museums, theaters, and restaurants were packed with celebrities for days before and after. Just previously, a prominent Arab terrorist had been freed by the French government, which caused some of the invited Americans to cable their objections and regrets. But refusals had little impact on the size of the invited crowd. There seemed to be a lot of art dealers and art critics especially.

A few days before the opening, one of Beaubourg's diagonal tensile members on the piazza side came loose—somebody had run a crane into it. The vertical elements hold the gerberettes down; the diagonal ones take care of wind, stability, and temperature movements. It looked worrying to guests, but one of the reasons the diagonals were unprotected against fire (and cranes) is that half of them could be lost without risk.

On the official opening night (as I remember, since it was my own first view of Beaubourg), the crowds were tremendous. The setting was dramatic as photographers flashlit evening-dressed guests on all levels, decks, and escalators. The doors closed at 8:20, regardless of who wasn't in. Président Giscard d'Estaing had decided that no refreshments would be served, but no one had mentioned this to the guests, so over 5,000 people spent fruitless hours trying to make their way from floor to floor looking for bars or buffets that didn't exist. (Richard Rogers later said to me that Madame Pompidou had had a more civilized earlier reception, at which she explained that the late president had found the project very beautiful. When he first saw the chosen winner, though, he had said to her, "*Ça va faire crier*"—that's going to cause an outcry.) By 9:30, there were mob scenes of people politely pushing and not getting any dinner. The ground floor was originally reserved for crowned heads and other dignitaries, but they pushed too. One partial vision of the huge building as a uniquely multi-story public place became clear: the multitudes on every level, controlled by attendants and guards, had the frightening aspect of a modern nightmare, out of *Metropolis* or *Dante's Inferno*.

When Giscard arrived, escalators were turned off or run the opposite way while security guards threw up temporary barriers and stopped people where they were. Giscard delivered a tribute to Pompidou, and a snub to Chirac, who didn't get to speak though he was mayor of Paris. There was no mention in Giscard's speech of the devoted client the Établissement Public, the designers, or the builders. With the work and the worry, it had been the worst day of all for the design team, and they wondered if after all they had built a political monument.

On February 2, the doors opened to the public for the first time. The crowds were as great as on the opening night every day for weeks; then they tailed off slightly but were averaging 20,000 people per Sunday (all of whom, of course, wouldn't have been inside at one time). In the first year, an estimated 6,000,000 persons visited Beaubourg, more than visited the Louvre and the Eiffel Tower put together. Of these, most were tourists, paying a single visit. The rest, about 1,200,000, about 90 percent French and 80 percent Parisian, were regular or occasionally repeating visitors, there primarily to use the cultural facilities of the Centre Pompidou.

The piazza. In early designs the basement levels were partly open to the sky

8   Meaning and influence

Press coverage of Beaubourg's opening was broad, and international. The newspapers on the whole were not sure whether to cover Beaubourg as political news, urban feature, or cultural criticism, and the filed stories tended to get published in that order when more than one reporter from a given paper arrived in Paris. The gist of commentary in the first flood was that the French were an odd people and they had got themselves an odd building. National characteristics were invoked to explain the Beaubourg phenomenon, such as the well-known French flamboyance, fashion consciousness, competitiveness against rival cultures, and willingness to embrace affected cultural or pseudocultural manifestations. Arts periodicals talked about the building as if it were all art gallery.

In France itself, a critical examination of Beaubourg's architectural and functional merits had been impossible to attempt for years because the building had become hopelessly intertwined with a dozen other issues, all remote from the question of architectural value. Unencumbered, Beaubourg could emerge for discussion—if ever—only after vituperative debate about urban resources, cultural resources, political gestures, and even architectural gestures. Beaubourg's apparent lack of design decorum might have contributed to the perception of it as a sort of problem child for the French media. It was easier to talk about the state of society than to settle on the question of whether Beaubourg was a misunderstood darling, or a juvenile delinquent.

To the hypersensitive Beaubourg designers and client body, their building seemed to inspire only hostility in France. Up to the opening, the press of the Right had been divided between those who hated Beaubourg for its apparent aim of institutionalizing contemporary culture, and those who were grudgingly prepared to respect it because it was Pompidou's fond dream, which might have some desirable impact. The Left press had been broadly against Beaubourg for its predicted effects of stultification and centralization, and because it allowed the government to ignore pressing cultural needs elsewhere, especially the need for libraries. It was thus a surprise in the first week of February 1977 to reread the same papers and see that Beaubourg had come through, journalistically speaking, and the towering waves of vilification had subsided to the merely choppy. Most of the popular papers remained hostile out of habit, but *Le Figaro* was circumspect, *Le Monde* appreciated Beaubourg aesthetically, and *L'Humanité,* the Communist paper, fully approved of Beaubourg and its aims.

In Britain, less notice was taken of the building, of course. But though the *Financial Times* got a good deal of detail wrong and the *Sunday Times* headlined Beaubourg "strangest building of the year," the *Sunday Telegraph* gave it a good review and interviewed Rogers. The art critic of the *Guardian* called Beaubourg "hideous" and suggested covering it with ivy or Virginia creeper, but the *Times* and *Evening Standard* were full of approval. In the British weeklies, the *New Statesman* was highly in favor,[1] and in the *Listener,* the architectural historian Mark Girouard took delight in describing the Rue de Renard side of the building as "a little like the back of a refrigerator, enormously enlarged, or a wireless when the back panel has been taken off." In the American press,

---

1 the *Evening Standard* piece ("French centre with a kick," February 1, 1977), the *New Statesman* article ("Monumental Gaul," February 11, 1977), and one in the U.S. *Harper's Magazine* ("Le Tour Babel," April 1977) were all by Nathan Silver. The three favorable pieces I wrote certainly didn't corner the market.

Beaubourg was looked upon as an art museum and was dealt with almost exclusively as an impertinent Paris effort to win back supremacy from New York as a center for painting and sculpture.

The architectural critics began to have their say. Some writers in the French professional magazine *L'Architecture d'Aujourd'hui* were vituperative, others favorable. Peter Cook, an architect member of the old Archigram group, thought Beaubourg was "where it's at," which was "a well equipped hangar." In the British *Architectural Review,* Reyner Banham suspected Beaubourg was the terminal monument of the "megastructure movement," about which he had written a recent book. He traced the concept of an adaptable stack of floors and considered the possibilities of "a permanent image of change," a preoccupation Banham dated from the Italian Futurists at the beginning of the century, but he came to no conclusion about that. Alan Colquhoun in *Architectural Design* magazine leveled more of an attack along similar lines. He seemed to accept the designers' belief about flexible looks at face value, as if one saw nothing but shimmering polymorphousness, and blamed the building for lacking culture as if it had no looks at all. Andrew Rabeneck in the same British magazine had a shrewder understanding of the designers' intentions: "If it could become whatever one wanted, then one must want it, Q.E.D."

Architecture is the most public art, and Beaubourg had become the most public of buildings. It rapidly generated its own critique as it began to prove useful. (Public opinion on obvious practicality is always approving.) The first predictable attitudes were undergoing transition, and by 1978 the press was deeply into more appreciative second thoughts about Beaubourg based on better knowledge, greater familiarity, and the news that people were voting with their feet. In particular, what had started at the outset as an almost accidental association of "library" with "arts center" was proving to be not only a workable relationship but a principled one, which would no doubt be widely copied.

But a worrying article that appeared then was by no outsider. It came out in *Libération,* the French independent Left paper, on the first anniversary of opening day, February 1, 1978. Its author was François Lombard, former head of the programmation group, whose piece was ferociously entitled *"Une Machine Grippée"* (a machine that has seized up). Lombard harshly criticized Beaubourg's financial and administrative management since its opening. He insisted that the wrong way to measure Beaubourg's success was by looking at the balance sheet. The right way was to judge "the quality and effectiveness of the service rendered," which he claimed was alarmingly bad:

> The personnel has changed from professionals to technocrats. . . . A sampling of staff today would reveal that many of them are unaware of the building's objectives, functions or activities. Thus the very first step has been lost.

Discussing his *Libération* article about a year later, Lombard was prepared to concede that Beaubourg was very tough on its staff because of the decision, for which he shared responsibility, to deliberately fragment activities to help public contact. When the general information desk was put at ground level, the detailed information on the second level, and more particular information for specialists at the other end of that level, the staff of experts were of course separated. Things for them were made more difficult, and it was slightly demoralizing. Misunderstood personnel become concerned only about themselves. But Beaubourg wasn't supposed to be a cultural center for the staff—museums sometimes become like that, Lombard said. Beaubourg should function extremely well as long as the management had faith in the idea of depending on the staff as promoters of a public information center. But Beaubourg's president, Jean Millier, had merged the points of public contact to promote efficiency without understanding the reasons for their distribution, in Lombard's view, and without much success in making the staff happier either.

This criticism of management from the recent program writer for the client called attention only to part of Beaubourg's problems. The restaurant on the fifth floor was a visible example of another. It was meant to offer the public cheap, relaxed, "nonelitist" meals and snacks, but it had both design and management shortcomings. A design difficulty was the problem of simply fitting such very demanding functions within a flexible building. At Beaubourg it was easy enough to accommodate offices, exhibition spaces, seating areas, and book stacks. Toilets had drainage and special ventilation requirements, but one such enclosure every 5,000 square meters or so presented few problems. But with a restaurant on the fifth level, the building was pushed to the extreme test of the flexibility principle; in allowing for food deliveries, reasonable acoustics, ventilation, and a dining atmosphere, its performance was uncomfortably stretched. The administrators made the situation worse by franchising the restaurant to an operator who normally did *autoroute* catering, so the food and service were undistinguished. Even the space was badly planned (always a risk in a truly flexible plan): inexplicable open areas lay beyond arbitrarily placed screens and canopies that seemed to have been introduced in a nervous attempt to create intimacy. Most of the furniture and equipment were provided to autoroute standards, not the Beaubourg designs. The restaurant seemed a prime example of Beaubourg's early administrative troubles.

Other examples were the lapses in building graphics, notices, and signs. Following the international graphic design competition, VDA, the winners, had produced an overall signing system for the building that had good style and the right scale. A few years later it wasn't being used properly. New signs were not being made regularly, as intended. At the Cinemathèque and elsewhere, small hand-written notices made program announcements. In a building devoted to information, the collapse of information design was a small but telling betrayal.

On the final architectural drawings for the ground floor eleven public entrances had been shown, for access into Beaubourg from all four sides. There was meant to be no "main" entrance; people were intended

With Beaubourg's
completion, the envisaged
pedestrian circulation across the
piazza was diminished by means
of fencing, and a management
decision to greatly reduce the
number of public entrances

to cross through the building if they wanted to, without stopping. The design team had hoped that neighborhood shoppers would take shortcuts through the ground floor and learn things en route. But a few years later, the north and south doors were blocked off to make room for more display space, thwarting the cross-circulation plan. To enter the building, most people needed to crowd around one small entrance on the piazza side, which also pushed a determined wedge of pedestrian circulation through the piazza. The management had actually reversed the important design concept of circulation by infiltration.

Disappointing management skepticism and ignorance (as the design team saw it) had kept the Nitzchke-like information screens off the building and the nonprogrammed activities unencouraged, but a consolation was that the latter was starting to happen anyway. After opening day Beaubourg's piazza had become public terrain, perpetually full of people, with events, participants, rings of viewers. The elevator housings on the back of the piazza became ad hoc performing stages. The big vents became poster display surfaces. A circus was allowed to set up its tent. The piazza was a success, but the crowds and the underestimated interest were producing problems of that success. Inside the building, replaceable architectural finishes such as carpets would have to be renewed more quickly than expected because of the influx of visitors. Most of the beautiful ash trays and coat hangers, purpose-made for Beaubourg, were pinched as souvenirs, and the wastebaskets were going fast. About 100 wire-structured Beaubourg chairs had been boldly loaded into a truck and stolen on opening day.

After handing over a building to a client, architects often feel like parents whose baby has left home, and Piano and Rogers were no exception. But they felt a right to be critical. Discussing organization problems, Renzo Piano thought the museum's setup was static and without participative bite. Architecturally he most regretted the loss of exterior space within the structural grid, the absence of information screens, and the loss of thorough transparency because of fire safety requirements. He especially missed the open ground floor with the building floating above half the piazza, though he admitted this might have been a Mediterranean notion, with daunting wind problems to solve if it had occurred. The early idea of adjustable-height floors had long been abandoned, but Piano felt that most of the spatial design variation possibilities that remained were not being used. Mezzanines had been developed for intermediate levels, but they were not used, and if a double height was wanted, a piece of floor was designed to be removable every two bays. Where was the flexible manipulation? As Piano explained,

> We have a book of rules for the client. There is a five-year transformability. Then there is a one-year transformability. And a one-week transformability: lightweight partitions. Even escalators can be turned around. The pieces can be interchanged. Beaubourg isn't built for 20 years, but for 300, 400, 500 years. That's the dimension. At first I was frightened by that. In a few years there could be another May 1968. We need to understand the permanence and the change. I hope the client understands too.

Other lessons were more easy for everyone to absorb, and for the client to feel proud of. Beaubourg's competition itself had enabled specific design intentions to be successful. The client had wisely chosen to be presented with a proper strategy as well as a design, and the jury had cleverly selected the one scheme above all that revealed strong strategic attitudes, the scheme's strategies promoting communications and flexibility. Moreover, the fair competition process that had been scrupulously followed had encouraged merit, with clear approval and a public viewing of the design at the outset. The achievement of the completed Beaubourg's remaining within the spirit of its first design would have remained obscure if the design team had received the job as a private commission and had developed it privately. The hair-raising yet effective process of public visibility and accountability throughout the making of Beaubourg was, among other things, a vindication of the competition method in architecture. It proved again that, when they work, competitions are the best way for new designers to break the hold of established architectural firms, and to popularize excellence.

Another valuable lesson was the Beaubourg team's operation, which became an unusually exposed example of a method of working on a modern building. It showed that though infighting among the design team was frequent, that was not very different from recorded examples of work on other jobs of equal complexity and size, done at high speed, with many innovative elements. Despite the crises, the method of work was efficient and effective. Stories about smoother-running projects of comparable size are generally to be found within more stable industrial or institutional frameworks—offshore oil structures, aircraft design—rather than in ad hoc teams recruited for one special purpose that have to start by inventing themselves. In that strangely parallel project to Beaubourg, the London Crystal Palace of 1851, the designer Joseph Paxton had great individual authority to enforce smooth working. But although the innovative spectrum Paxton dealt with was broad (Paxton effectively originated metal and glass building construction), it was far less deep and less testing than the thousands of abstruse technological puzzles that had to be solved at Beaubourg. To compare the P & R–Arup design team to Paxton's, or Eiffel's, actually points up the differences: the contemporary design team seems inevitably more fractious and less brilliant by comparison, and, lacking the discipline of the solitary leader, exhibits internal dissention that causes periods of indecisiveness and low morale. But countering this, even a modest modern technological building is usually beyond the scope of a brilliant single generalist. The Beaubourg design wasn't conceivably encompassable by one person, but in execution it nevertheless managed to convey a sense of clear control of the sort provided by leadership, not committee compromise. This was a sovereign achievement.

The design process at Beaubourg thus sheds light on the major problem of many complex contemporary buildings, especially where technology is an important factor: how to make rational decisions among all the choices. The sometimes incapacitating work problem was how not to arrive at grand flights of fancy. So it was fortuitous (or very cunning) that Beaubourg was designed to express simplicity, despite its complex wherewithal, and despite the fact that it never became really simple. In this way, Beaubourg started to achieve the hierarchy of complexity-within-simplicity of a Gothic building such as Chartres (to which it was occasionally poetically compared in the favorable French periodicals), rather than the exalted and excluding formal simplicity of the London Crystal Palace or classical buildings such as the Rome Pantheon.

Finally, there was the issue to settle of how it looked, and where that came from. Was Beaubourg's "flexibility look," its supposedly sheer expression of dynamic contingency, an adequate explanation of how it does look? There is little evidence that the competition jury was concerned with appearances at the time: its report said the winner used daylight well, left an open public space, was functional rather than merely monumental, and offered an approach to a modern progressive interpretation of culture by presenting it as "information." Juror Philip Johnson later recalled[2] that he was attracted by the actual looks of the submission, in terms of the "all hang-out atmosphere" of the exterior mechanical equipment and the "wavy lines" of the escalators, but principally he was for it because "it was the only entry likely to be built, since the users could design their own spaces within the framework." That long odds were reckoned against anything actually being built was a "jury secret" its members kept strictly to themselves, Johnson commented. Yet history shows that whatever the jury's expectations (or lack of them) about eventual looks, the design's functional, flexible, polyvalent demonstration paid off at once in the most practical way: by inciting the willingness to go ahead.

Although the Geste Architecturale and a few architecture critics later saw this flexibility as a refusal to consider looks, an abdication of an

---

2 In a telephone interview with the author, 1978.

architect's most enshrined responsibility, Beaubourg of course was given a settled, self-evident form. There were trepidations about this within the design team. Alan Stanton noticed that as they worked toward opening day, they found they were "falling in love with the details" (his phrase recalled the Arup engineer's mockery about the team falling in love with the problems). According to Stanton, the architects did try to keep this from happening, and attempts were made not to "lose spontaneity." There was overt concern about the building becoming designed instead of properly offhand. But they couldn't help it. Finally, despite all denial, there it was, as it had to be: a composition. Despite the polymorphic ideals, specificity was still inevitable. Beaubourg had to stop being everything or anything, and become something—a particular form for a certain period of time. Flexibility as the encompassing idea had to give over to adaptability—a merer, less than total, arrangement.

Su Rogers, one of the original partners in the competition, was ambivalent about the way the design turned out. She agreed Beaubourg was an important building because she doubted that exposed surfaces and exposed steel structure could be taken much further. She admired it for its consistency and felt there was no compromise in it. But although she admired its "determinism," she criticized that too. She suspected that the flexibility proposition went too far where it didn't count—in enormous spans and technical extravagances—and not far enough where it would have mattered in making things more suitable for their uses, for example, in providing better exhibition space for paintings. Simply having the space to put a building within a building in order to view paintings struck her as an irrational approach.

Was Beaubourg's particular design intention of uninterrupted space too uncompromising? If there had been, say, a row of columns down the center, the building would have been just as flexible; perhaps four soccer matches might not have been playable on every floor, but the truss girder depth would have been half, and building costs probably

On the floors of the Musée National d'Art Modeme, the structural elements were comparatively shrouded by the museum planners so the artworks would have the principal visual impact

less than that. But Renzo Piano looked back and was glad that they had maintained clear principles:

> Once you put the column in the center, it doesn't only mean to put the column. Then it becomes perfectly logical to put one lift, and maybe some pipes. It's perfectly logical. Then you put centrally all the system of feeding the building. This other building may be fantastic, I don't know. But in a sense, our building's quality, its value, is in its extremity.

Beaubourg's extremity gave it no predetermined looks, but a rhetoric not difficult to infer from the long- or short-term composition of its exterior. To most who visit it, it is a dazzling or frightening assemblage of enormous vitality and perhaps baffling complexity; a raw symbol of violent newness. First there is the visceral reaction, which precious few buildings in the world have elicited. Afterward, the formal language speaks in terms of familiar culture: "high technology" and "petrochemical industry," probably, followed by "style of the future," and perhaps "Museum of Modern Art–approved." It also says "contrasts can be good," and "blending with the surroundings doesn't always matter." To architects, it may say "flexible and indeterminate," if they have read up. In other buildings too, the search for flexibility and indeterminacy has often, somewhat paradoxically, achieved strong, commanding forms: Buckminster Fuller's "flexible" domes (where the users have to demonstrate flexibility, not the domes); Le Corbusier's Algiers viaduct housing (a permitted diversity of apartments within overriding unity); the "megastructure" designs of recent years where structure held sway over infill, as Beaubourg also showed.

To its architectural advocates and theorists in the 1960s, the idea of "megastructure,"[3] undeniably an influence on Beaubourg, was that a structural framework could be developed that would be replicated, would spread, and would finally take over. One was even postulated in mid-air above historic Paris, accessible via elevators shooting up within the very, very high-rise columns. The megastructurists

---

3 See Reyner Banham, *Megastructure, Urban Futures of the Recent Past* (London 1976).

supposed that by such designs, cities would become a single building. Beaubourg had the massive overall framework appropriate to the task, but it was not a megastructure design according to the defining distinction, since Beaubourg was never conceived as the beginning of a new city form to spread and prevail. It was rather an overt, almost shattering contrast with the city around it, whose effect—like that of the medieval cathedrals—depended on the city's never becoming like it. Its difference of form and scale (really, its monumentality) was one of its most remarkable and original qualities, reinforced by its site planning to keep open space around it.

So in stylistic terms, Beaubourg helped close a tradition and tentatively offered the beginning of what comes after. On its tradition-ending side, the design theories of functionalism still conclusively held sway for its makers, not the question of looks. The notion that "logic" and "research" should fashion architecture was very much in their hearts, and Beaubourg's looks, for them, were an almost inadvertent supervention. On the tradition-beginning side, the visible forms were eloquent. They conveyed a rational and satisfying sense of a developing architectural culture, and not just how air is moved or glass is shaded.

Indeed, the developing architectural culture of the early 1970s was converging. Between 1972 and 1974, architects who knew nothing of the Beaubourg competition at the firm of Perry, Dean and Stewart in Boston were designing the Wellesley College Science Center, a multi-story concrete building with its structure, ductwork, and piping for various services placed outside and color coded so they could easily be modified according to changing research needs. The Wellesley Science Center was completed in September 1975, and it looks like Beaubourg's unacknowledged sibling in concrete and fiberglass.[4] Designing for flexibility as an intentionally adhocist mode was

---

4 Wellesley Science Center's partner in charge was Charles F. Rogers (no relation to Richard), and the project architect was Robert Silver, my brother, now a partner of Schwartz/Silver Architects in Boston. My brother confirms that no one working on Wellesley had yet seen or heard of the Beaubourg design, which scarcely had more than its primary steel up when Wellesley was finished.

certainly in the air, and Beaubourg was its most important built manifestation.

As for future influence, Beaubourg may lead somewhere new, but it is too early to tell yet. Its looks, ironically, could be its most influential aspect. It has become such a famous building that this fact alone makes its influence an uncertain benefit. Like the winning design of the Boston City Hall competition of 1961 , following which half the towns in America got little Boston City Halls gracing their civic centers and shopping centers, many diluted Beaubourgs will probably erupt in cities all over the world in the decades to come—especially since *tripes* on the outside means open spaces on the inside, as handy for office buildings as for information centers and science centers. Certainly a small number of derivatives will be engagingly much brasher; thefts will produce more interesting further developments; real progress won't be thwarted.

The least that can be said for Beaubourg stylistically is that it provided the world with the missing archetype of the ultratechnological aesthetic. This countered the stylistic interests of the rival architectural camp of the day, concerned mainly with historical allusion (otherwise known as "blending in," or "just having good manners" as Prince Charles put it in 1988, when he decided to remind the world about architectural decorum). Beaubourg gave heart to the previously less popular side, even helping to advance an egregious "high-tech" fashion. The most that can be said for it is that it started to do its job. Its job was to be a reincarnation of authoritative French visual culture, a rebirth-mark of national optimism, a monument for our time, and (not least) a day trip for the family. All of this may in the end prove to have been completely accomplished, but as Piano suspected, it may be 200 or 300 years too early to know.

In *Mont-Saint-Michel and Chartres* (1905), the American Henry Adams tried to explain the life and art that had informed those two great French monuments built by teams of people. A lot of fiction is in

Adams, as we know; yet his truth is closer, one often feels, than could ever be discerned in plain history. There is a passage where Adams describes the design innovations of Chartres, and with the difference of the specifically Christian precept, it might stand for Beaubourg:

> The architect at Chartres was required by the Virgin to provide more space for her worshippers within the church. . . . That this order came directly from the Virgin may be taken for granted. At Chartres, one sees everywhere the Virgin, and nowhere any rival authority; one sees her give orders, and architects obey them—but very rarely a hesitation as though the architect were deciding for himself. In his western front, the architect has obeyed orders so literally that he has not even taken the trouble to apologise for leaving unfinished the details which, if he had been responsible for them, would have been his anxious care.
>
> ...The work shows blind obedience, as though he were doing his best to please the Virgin without trying to please himself.

The obedience at Beaubourg was to the principle of innovation and change. Whatever following Beaubourg ultimately begets, its basis will probably lie less in Beaubourg's purpose, style, or imposing looks than in this innovative spirit it plainly proclaims, without the architect's hesitation or apology. More than the winning ways of any contemporary design formula, that spirit radiates at Beaubourg, and is truly a higher thing.

Appendix: Beaubourg's credits

1	Client:	Établissement Public, Centre Nationale d'Art et de Culture Georges Pompidou
	President	Robert Bordaz
	Project director	Sébastien Loste
	Finance and administration	Claude Mollard
	Construction	André Darlot, Gérard Rigadeau, Jean-Marc Prudhomme
	Program	François Lombard, Claude Pecquet, Patrick O'Byrne, Jacques Lichnerowicz
	Department of plastic arts (CNAM)	Pontus Hulten, Germain Viatte
	Public information library (BPI)	Jean-Pierre Seguin
	Industrial design center (CCI)	François Mathey

Institute for the research and coordination of acoustics and music (IRCAM)	Pierre Boulez
Furniture	Michel Vaniscotte
Exhibitions	Henri Bouilhet
Audiovisual	Pierre Tailhardat

2	Architects:	Piano & Rogers
	Partners in charge	Renzo Piano and Richard Rogers
	Substructure and mechanical equipment	Walter Zbinden with Hans-Peter Bysaeth, Johanna Lohse, Peter Merz, Philippe Dupont
	Superstructure and mechanical services	Laurie Abbott with Shunji Ishida, Hiroshi Naruse, Hiroyuki Takahashi
	Facades and galleries	Eric Holt with Michael Davies, Jan Sircus
	Competition, program, interiors	Gianfranco Franchini
	Internal/external systems, audiovisuals	Alan Stanton with Michael Dowd, William Logan, Noriaki Okabe, Rainer Verbizh
	Environment and piazza, scenographic spaces	Cuno Brullmann
	Coordination and site supervision	Bernard Plattner

IRCAM	Michael Davies with Noriaki Okabe, Ken Ruppard, Jan Sircus, Walter Zbinden
Secretarial	Françoise Gouinguenet, Claudette Spielmann and Colette Valensi
Furniture	John Young with François Barat, Helène Diebold, Jacques Fendard, Jean Huc, Helga Schlegel

3   Engineers: Ove Arup and Partners

Partners in charge	Povl Ahm, Edmund Happold, Peter Rice, Gerry Clarke
Structure	Edmund Happold, Peter Rice, Lennart Grut, Rob Pierce
Air conditioning	Tom Barker, Bernard Legrand, Bryn James
Electricity	Alain Bigan, Vincent Randazzo
Plumbing	Daniel Lyonnet
Consultant	Cabinet Trouvin
Cost control	Marc Espinoza, Denis Stone, Frazer MacIntosh, Malek Grundberg
Transportation	Michael Sargent
Project planning	Harry Saridjin

4	Management contractor:	Grands Travaux de Marseilles (GTM)
	Job engineer	Jean Thaury

5	Main contractors:	
	Structure	Krupp
	Structure	Pont à Mousson
	Structure	Pohlig
	Facades	CFEM
	Elevators and escalators	Otis
	Secondary structure	Voyer
	Mechanical equipment	Industrielle de Chauffage
	Mechanical equipment	Saunier Duval
	Mechanical equipment	CGEE Alsthom
	Fire protection	Cape International
	Stage and studio equipment	Sores
	Fluorescent lighting	CETEK
	Elevator motor room housings	Lafoucrière
	Museum lighting systems	Concord

Index

The heterogeneous subject matter of a building biography has provoked a few liberties in indexing. As even the institutional divisions of Beaubourg have multiple designations, most associations are indexed by acronym. French titles, words, and macaronic phrases that were used in preference to English have been likewise given priority in the index (e.g., En charette; Programmation group). Throughout, explanatory words in brackets have sometimes been added, and some duplicate references have been provided.

A reference to be found within a footnote is indicated with an f after the page number (e.g., 15f). A reference to an illustration or picture caption is indicated in square brackets. A reference to a name appearing in the Appendix credit list is indicated merely with Appx.

Aalto, Alvar, 41, 103
Abbott, Laurie, 62, 97, 145, 148, 149, 150, 151,
    152, Appx
Academicians, French, 155
Acoustical consultants, 165
Acoustics and music institute. *See* IRCAM
Acrylic, 20, 160
"Activity sandwich," 156
Adams, Henry, 187
Adaptability, 24, [34], 45, 88, 103, 162, 175, 183.
    See also Flexibility
Adhocism. *See* Improvisation
Administration of Centre, x, 176–177
    and staff, 176
Aerospace. *See* Space program

Architects. *See* Piano & Rogers
Aesthetic convictions, 22, 145, 187
Ahm, Povl, 7, 74, 83, 92, 112, 115f, Appx
Aillaud, Émile, 27
Air conditioning, 87, 103, 127, 140, 145, 146,
    148, 152, 158. *See also* Mechanical
    equipment
Algiers viaduct housing, 185
Algerians, 131
Aluminum, 140, 149, 160
America
    and Vietnam, 3
    man-made, 21
American(s), 149, 170
    principles of design, 21–22

Americans *(Continued)*
    runners-up in competition, 41
Amiens, 9
Amsterdam, 27
Anechoic chambers, 126
Anglo-Italians, 58, 131
Anglophiles, 53
Anglo-Saxons, 154
Anti-Gaullists, 4
Appleby, Sally, 47
APD (avant projet detaillé), 76
APS (avant projet sommaire), 58, 59, 60–61, 62, 66,
    72, 76, 80, 106, 110
    wedding-cake structure ("the jelly-mold
        scheme," "the Pompidou section"), 61
ARAM, 16
Archigram group, 25, 61, 175
Architectural Association School of Architecture
    (London), 6, 62
Architectural Design, 175
Architectural draftsmen, 92
Architectural models, 60, 92, 124, 145, 146, 150,
    151, 152
Architectural plans kept fluid, 94–95
Architectural presentation technique, 32
Architectural Review, The, 175
Architectural traditions, 186–187
Architectural value of Centre, 173
Architecture d'Aujourd'hui, L', 175
Articulation, 44
Art museum. *See* CNAM
Arts lab, 105
Arup. *See* Ove Arup and Partners
Arup, Ove, 48
Atmosphere, 177, 182
Audiovisual presentation, 162, 164
Australians, 62
Austria, 14–15f
Autoroute catering, 177
Avant projet detaillé. *See* APD
Avant projet sommaire. *See* APS
Axonometrics. *See* Drawings

Baltard, Victor, 1, 2, 124
Banham, Reyner, 175, 185f
Barat, François, Appx

Barclay, Michael, 14, 62, 70–71f, 115f
Barge, 92
Barker, Tom, 64, 94, 115, 145, 146, 148, Appx
Barré, François, 11
Barrettes, 118
Barrow-in-Furness (U.K.), 30
Basement construction. *See* Substructure
BDS (British Development Standard), 121–122
Bearings, 133, 134
Beaubourg
    as familiar name of building, ix, 11, 168
    institutional users' accommodation within, ix,
        22–23
    as name of site and district, ix, 1, 2
    neighborhood of, 102
    project manager of (*see* Bordaz)
    as tourist attraction, x, 102
Belfast, 8
Benefactors, 160
Berlinoise retaining wall, 118
BET (Bureau d'Études Techniques), 60, 69–70, 72
Bibliothèque des Halles proposal, 2
Bidonville, 131
Bigan, Alain, Appx
Blanchard, John, 138
Blot, M., 137
Boccaccio, 1
Bookstacks, 162
Bordaz, Robert, 12, 13, 49, 54, 55, 57, 60, 73, 74,
    86, 94, 112, 114, 115, 124, 125, 150,
    151, 155, 159, Appx
Boss (tension tie node), [84], 134
Boston City Hall, 187
Bouilhet, Henri, Appx
Boulez, Pierre, 58, 125, 165, Appx
BPI (library), ix, x, 10, 24, 43, 104, 156, 158, 162
Brancusi, Constantin, 162
Britain, 32, 51, 88, 121, 174. *See also* England
    National Strike of, 3
British, 124
    construction gangs, 131
    professional contracts, 81–82
    working method in building, 58, 69
British Development Standard. *See* BDS
British Museum, 27
Brittleness (of steel), 122

Brown, David, xiii

Brullmann, Cuno, Appx

Budget cut. *See* Cancellation crisis

Budget for Beaubourg. *See* Building budget

Builders of Beaubourg, 171

Building biography, xii

Building budget, 80–81, 89, 112, 123, 126, 139, 146, 158, 162, 163, 164, [167], 169, 170

Building Design Partnership, 15f

Building finishes, 104, 149, 150

Building industry, 29, 78, 95. *See also* French, building industry

Building services. *See* Mechanical equipment

Building site. *See* Sitework

Building's looks, 139, 157, 175, 182, 185, 187

Building volume, 32, 100, 101, 117, 126, 156–157

Bureau de Controle, 99, 119

Bureau d'Études Techniques. *See* BET

Burrell Gallery (Glasgow competition), 15, 16

Business loans, 66

Bysaeth, Hans-Peter, Appx

Cabinet Trouvin, 146, Appx

Cables, 143, 150

Cabray, Colonel, 137, 138

Cafe, x, [109], 177

California, 62, 63, 91, 163

Cambridge (UK), 15

Cancellation crisis, 123–125, [167]

Cannes Film Festival, 12

Cantilever beams. *See* Steel, gerberettes

Capacity of building, public, 137, 140

Cape International, Appx

Capoflex, 141

Carmen, Bill, 63

Carpet, 27, 140

Cast iron, 1

Catering, 177

Catwalks, [157], 164

CCI (le Centre de Création Industrielle), ix, x, 10, 44

Centre du Plateau Beaubourg. *See* Beaubourg

Centre Nationale d'Art et de Culture Georges Pompidou. *See* Centre Pompidou

Centre Pompidou, as name later given, ix, [xiv], 168, 172

CETEK, Appx

CFEM, 143, Appx

CGEE Alsthom, Appx

Champs Élysées, 32

Channel tunnel, 4

Charge calorifique, 137–138

Charles de Gaulle airport, 4

Charpy v-notch test, 122

Chartres, 182, 187–188

Chauvinism, 65, 114, 154, 155

Checking, 146

Chelsea Football Club, 13, 14

Chicago, 20

Children's library, ix

Children's workshop, ix

Chirac, Jacques, 171

Chromium, 122

Cinakothèque, 141, 162

Cinemathèque Française, x, 177

Circulation
    on exterior galleries, 31, [144], [178]
    pedestrian, 25, 31, 44, 59, [178], 179

Cladding. *See* Curtain wall

Clarke, Gerry, 14, 86, 115, 115f, 170, Appx

Client
    administrative structure of, 11–13, 73, 8–79, 97–101
    confidence in architects and engineers, 61, 90, 151, 154
    construction group, 79, 98–99
    contracts with architects and engineers (*see* Contracts, professional)
    Établissement Public du Centre Beaubourg (including earlier name, "la Délégation pour la realisation du Centre du Plateau Beaubourg"), 12, 54, 55, 57, 72, 77, 78, 79, 80, 92, 98, 114, 119, 123, 124, 151, 154, 156, 164, 168, 171, 174, 180, Appx
    handing over the building to, 179
    institutional user group (representatives of museum, library, etc.), 78, 79, 156, 165, 169, [184]
    programmation group, 10, 11, 49, 58, 78, 79, 93, 94, 100–101, 103, 104, 125, 177
    working method with architects and engineers, 75, 79

CNAM (modern art museum), ix, 10, 24, 43, 104,

CNAM (Continued)
124, [144], 151, 156, 160–162, 169, 176, 179, [184]
"Collusion" of bidders, 112–114
Color coding, 150, 151, 152, [153], 160, 186
Color expert, 151
Colors, [128], 150–154, 159
Colquhoun, Alan, 175
Combustibility. See Fire safety
Communications architecture, [128], 180
Communication problems, 121–122, 149, 166. See also Language barrier
Competition
    American runners-up in, 41
    announcement for, 13
    benefits of, 154, 180–181
    decision to hold, 4, 10
    design decisions for (see Design of Beaubourg)
    as an experience in research, 17
    general disadvantages of a, 14–15, 15f, 101, 103
    jury, 26–28, 38, 49, 93, 94, 154, 180
    jury deliberations, 38–42
    "market research" on jury members during, 26–28
    other contestants of, 26, 39, 41, 50
    prize money, 40, 41, 53
    program/brief for, 22–24
    report of jury, xiii, 42–47, 154, 182
    submission, 32, 35–37, 163
    supplanting the winners of, fears about, 48, 51 (see also Ove Arup and Partners, fears of being supplanted)
    time spent on, 31
    winners' experiences, 48–55, 57
Completion date, 166–168, 169
Complexity, 21, 24, 46, 166, 182, 185
Computers, 93, 126, 165
Concord, Appx
Concorde (supersonic plane), 4
Concrete, 20, 27, 29, 68, 117, 118, 132, 135, 186
    as bogus alternative material for superstructure, 113
Conference rooms, 126, 141
Conflict of interest, 77
Construction
    costs, 58, 72, 73, 76, 80, 103, 112–114, 125,

131, 139, 149, 164, 165, 168, 169, 183 (see also Building budget)
    delivery, assembly, and erection, 27, 88, [111], 122, 123, 126, 129, 131–132, [133], 137, 154, 156
    ease of, 26, 44, 123
    environmental impact of, 25, 131
    final costs of, 169–170
    timetable, 30, 49, 58, 88–90, 103, 130, 131, 132, 139, 143, 165, 166, 168, 169
Contingency margin of budget, 73, 169–170
Contractors, 80, 93, 118, 148, 150, 166. See also French, contractors
Contracts, building, 130
Contracts, professional, 54–55, 57–58, 59, 72–75, 78, 169
    and the contract accepted, 73
    and legal liabilities, 75
    and penalties, 73, 74 (see also Contingency margin of budget)
Convoi exceptionnel, 132
Cook, Peter, 175
Cooling towers, 148, 154
Cornell (University), 8, 62
Cosco, Giovanni, 41
Cost control, 93, 103, 112, 118, 170
Cost effectiveness, 103
Cost of construction. See Construction, costs
Couleuriste, 151
Chrysalis, 63
Crack growth, 121
Craftsmanship, 87, 95
Crane, tower, 132
Crises, 169, 181
Critical path analyses, 118, 166
Criticism. See Design of Beaubourg, critical appreciation; Design of Beaubourg, antipathy to
Crystal Palace (London and New York), 67, 181, 182
Crystal transformation (in tempered steel), 122
CSTB (fire safety authority), 99, 137, 138, 139, 160
"Cultural supermarket," 155
Culture, 102, 105, 174, 175, 182
Culture center, 26, 102, 172, 176
Curtain wall, 143, [147]

Custom design, 21

Danish, 124
Darlot, André, 13, 79, 98, Appx
Davies, Mike, 60, 62, 63, 125, 165, Appx
Dawson, Chris, 60, 62, 63
Dead load, 132
De Gaulle, Charles, 2
Défense, La, 4
Délégation pour la realisation du Centre du Plateau
     Beaubourg. *See* Client
Deliveries, 177
Département des Arts Plastiques. *See* CNAM
Department of Plastic Arts. *See* CNAM
Design consistency, 70, 159, 183
Design control, 58, 102, 103, 118, 150
Designed look, the [120], 183
Design intentions, x, 19–22, 129, 180
Design of Beaubourg
     antipathy to, 50, 58, 93, 154–155, 174–175,
          182–183
     archetypes, 25, 32 (*see also* Archigram
     group; Nitzchke, Oscar)
     competition entry, 24–26, 31–33, 157
     competition judging criteria, 39
     critical appreciation of, 125, 173, 174–175
     decorum of, 174, 187
     designer-maker relationship in, 95–97, 118
     detailing of, 123, 132, 150
     development of, 60–61, 63, 96, 129–131, 169
     importance of, 62
     jury's appreciation of, 44–47
     precepts (*see* Piano & Rogers, design precepts for
          Beaubourg)
     program changes to, 79, 89, 100–101, 156, 158,
          159, [167], 169, 170
     revisions to, 146, 156
     structural, 126 (*see also* Ove Arup and Partners;
          Steel)
Design options, 35
Design problems in Centre, 177, 179
Design process, xi, 95, 118, 129–131, 139, 168,
     181–182
Design Research Unit, 16
Design team, 79, 86, 99, 124, 147, 150, 166, 168,
     169, 171, 174, 179, 181. *See also* Ove Arup

and Partners; Piano & Rogers
Diebold, Helène, Appx
Dienbienphu, 12
Dimensions of building, 133
Display equipment and furnishing, 159
Docks, 30
Document Techniques Unifie. *See* DTU
Dowd, Michael, Appx
Drawings, 130, 145, 146, 148, 150, 168, 177. *See*
     also Architectural plans kept fluid;
     Architectural presentation technique;
     Competition, submission
DTU (Document Techniques Unifié), 119
Ductwork, 144, 149, 151, 161. *See also* Mechanical
     equipment
Dugdale, Tony, 60, 62, 66
Dupont, Philippe, Appx

East, Nathaniel, 41
Eccentric loads, [107], 134. *See also* Steel, columns
École des Beaux-Arts, 71, 154
Economic commitment, 131
Economic slump, 113
Eiffel, Alexandre Gustave, 181
Eiffel Tower, 30, 151, 155, 172
Electrical equipment, 87, 104, 140, 145, 146, 148,
     149, 150, 152, [153]
Electrician, 150
Electrographic displays, 32, 101, 104
Electrostatic application of finishes, 149
Elevation, eastern, [18], 26, [120], [128], [142],
     [153]
Elevation, southern, [136], 163
Elevation, western, [viii], 26, [56], [98], [107],
     [133], [147], [161], [178]
Elevations, provisional, 94–95
Elevators, 25, 32, 44, 96–97, 110, 126, 127, 139,
     140, 145, 149, 152, [153]
Elias, Ruth. *See* Rogers, Ruth
Elitism, 4, 16, 102, 177
Élysée Palace, 52, 125, 126
En charette, 35
Energy, 150
Engineers. *See* Ove Arup and Partners
England, 25, 48, 86. *See also* Britain
English character, 21, 60

Entrances, 24, 177, [178], 179

Environmental control, 103, 117

Epoxy, 160

Esalen, 91

Escalators, [xiv], 32, 33, [34], 44, 45, [56], 104,
    [107], 109–110, 111, 144, 152, [161],
    171, 180, 182

Espace de Projection, 126, 165

Espinoza, Marc, Appx

Établissement Public. *See* Client

Europe, x, 4, 74, 90, 97, 100, 117

Evening Standard, The, 174, 174f

Excavation, 44, 89, 118, 126

Excellence, 27, 181

Exhibition halls, 25

Exits, 137, 140

Expansion joints, 134

Expression, 108

Expressionism, 42

Expo 67. *See* Montreal

Expo 70. *See* Osaka

Extension of time, 166

Exterior display. *See* Screen, information

Facade. *See* Elevation; Piano & Rogers, facades and
    galleries team

Facade activities. *See* Electrographic displays; Screen,
    information

Factory finish, 149

False facade, 25

Fantastic buildings, 25

Farber, Manny, 148

Fast tracking, 89–90, 117, 169

Fees, professional, 16, 51, 57, 58, 59, 72, 75, 78,
    81–83, 139, 169, 170

Fences on piazza, [178]

Fendard, Jacques, Appx

Ferrous construction, 67. *See also* Cast iron; Steel

Festival of Britain (London 1951), 7

Fiberglass, 20, 186

Fifth Republic, 2, 4

Figaro, Le, 174

Financial Times, The, 174

Finish. *See* Building finishes

Fire
    active systems for, 140, [153], 162

collapse in, 139, 140, 141, 143

passive systems for, 141, 160

protection coatings, 138, 141

ratings, 140, 141

safety, [18], 44, 67, 100, 126, 137–143, [144],
    149, 158, 159, 160, 169, 171, 180

wall, 139, [142]

First Empire, 2

Flack, Peter, 31, 47

Flats (movable screens), 161

Flexibility, x, 20, 21, 24, 30, 31, 44, 45, 61, 63,
    103, 104, 126, 143, 145, 159, 165, 175, 177,
    180, 182, 183, 185

Floor area, 103, 108, 169

Floor levels
    movable, 30, 58, 180
    number of, 26, 117, 125, 126, 175

Forum, 156, [157]

Foster, Norman, 6, 62

Foster, Wendy, 6

Foundry, founders, [116], 132, 134

Fracture mechanics, 121

Fragmenting activities in Centre, 176

France, 121
    Commune of, 3
    Conseiller d'État of, 12
    Council of Ministers of, 3
    cultural maturity of, 154
    living in, 66, 114 (*see also* Paris, living in)
    Ministry of Cultural Affairs (Ministère des
        Affaires Culturelles) of, 8, 9, 10, 11, 42, 80,
        93, 124
    Ministry of Finance (Ministère de l'Economie) of,
        73, 80
    Ministry of National Education (Ministère de
        l'Education Nationale) of, 42
    working in, 15, 59

Franchini, Gianni, 17, 19, 31, 41, 47, 48, 52, 53,
    59, 60, 65, 66, 79, 151, 159, Appx

Francis, Sir Frank, 27

French
    architects, 85, 123–124, 154–155
    architectural institute (Ordre des Architectes), 78
    banks, 66
    building industry, 29, 68, 76, 77, 87, 119, 154
    building regulations, 89, 99, 119 (*see also*

French *(Continued)*
    SOCOTEC)
    clients, 119
    contractors, 51, 71, 80, 85, 86, 114
    Embassy, London, 36
    fire safety requirements (*see* CSTB)
    government, 170
    legal liability in design and construction, 71, 75
        (*see also* Insurance, professional liability)
    modern architecture, 71
    national characteristics, 154, 173
    press, 154–155, 182 (*see also* Press coverage)
    professional fees, 70
    speaking, 50, 62, 65, 83
    visual culture, 187
    working method in building, 58, 60, 69–72, 76, 86
Fuller, Buckminster, 28, 185
Fumel (France), 134
Fun Palace, 25
Function, 101, 188
Functional planning, 110
Functionalism, 22, 45, [120], 182, 186
Furniture, 101, 149, 151, 159, 162, 168, 177, 179
Futurists, 175

Gabo, Naum, 27
Galbreath, Samuel, 41
Galleries, exterior, 32, 33, 92, 104, [144], 144, [147]. *See also* Piano & Rogers, facades and galleries team
Galvanized steel, 149
Gare de Lyon, 30
Gaullist party, 3, 123, 125
GECO (Groupement des Enterprises), 119
Geometry, 31, 43, 44
Genoa, 5, 20, 28, 31, 37, 47, 59, 83
Geodesic domes, 28, 185
Gerber, Heinrich, 106f
Germany, and Germans, 13, 106, 113, 124, 131, 132, 163
Geste Architecturale, La, 154, 182
Girouard, Mark, 174
Giscard d'Estaing, Valèry, 123, 124, 125, 126, 127, 154, 165, 169, 171
Glasgow, 15

Glass, 1, 126, 139, [147], 148, 181
Goldschmied, Marco, 6, 19, 31, 35, 59, 63
Gouinguenet, Françoise, Appx
"Grand Beaubourg," 125, 126
Grand Palais, 50, 52, 55, 92
Grands Travaux de Marseille, Les. *See* GTM
Graphics for Centre, 159, 177
Grassin, M., 87
Grenoble, 9
Ground slab, 118
Groupement des Enterprises. *See* GECO
Grundberg, Malek, Appx
Grut, Lennart, 7, 64, 83, 86, 94, 113, 115, 122, 170, Appx
GTM (management contractor), 77, 80, 85–88, 93, 113, 114, 130, 166, 168
Guardian, The, 174
Guests at official opening, 170, 171
"Guts" (mechanical equipment), 25, 148, 187

Halles, Les, 1, 2, 124, 125
Handing over the building to the client, 179
Happold, Edmund (Ted), xiii, 7, 8, 13, 14, 16, 19, 26, 28, 29, 30, 31, 47, 48, 49, 50, 51, 52, 53, 54, 55, 58, 59, 68, 70–71f, 74, 83, 90, 112, 114, 115, 115f, Appx
Harper's Magazine, 174f
Harrisburg (Pennsylvania), 5
Heat gain, 103
Heating, 104, 145
Heat treatment. *See* Tempering
Heave (uplift force), 118
Heckel Blaihart, 134
Height restrictions, 100, 125, 169
Henkel, David, 138
High-tech fashion, 187
Hill, Jim, 91
Historical allusion, 187
Hoggett, Peter, xiii
Holt, Eric, 62, 149, Appx
Huc, Jean, 159, Appx
Huffman, Richard, 41
Hulten, Pontus, 124, 151–152, 156, 158, 160, 163, [184], Appx
Humanité, L', 174
"Humanizing" technology, 150

Hydraulic force. *See* Uplift

Ice skating, 162
Iconography, 32–33
Imperial College (London), 8
Improvisation, 19–20, 94–95, 186–187
Indian, 131
Indoor garden, 156
Industrial architecture, [128]
Industrial components, use of, 21
Industrial design center of Beaubourg. *See* CCI
Industrielle de Chauffage, Appx
Inflatable structure, 91, 92, 104
Influence of Beaubourg, 176, 187
Information
    concept for Beaubourg, x, 10, 33, 104, 177, 182
    hung or projected on the structure, 32, 33, 44,
        162–164 (*see also* Electrographic displays;
        Screen, information)
Innovative proposals and methods, 27, 72, 181,
    187–188
Institut de Recherches et de Coordination
    Acoustique/Musique, l'. *See* IRCAM
Institut de Soudure, l', 114
Institute for acoustics and music. *See* IRCAM
Insulation, 143, 149
Insurance, fire and flood, for Centre, 119
Insurance, professional liability, 78, 169. *See also*
    French, legal liability in design and
    construction
Interiors, 139, [157], 159, 160, 169, [184]
Intermediate levels. *See* Mezzanine
International Union of Architects, 13
Interpreter, 52, 92
Intumescent paint, 141, 143
Invention, 22
IRCAM (l'Institut de Recherches et de Coordination
    Acoustique/Musique), ix, 58, 64, 100, 101,
    119, 125–126, 165–166, [167], 169
    additions built in 1989 to, [167]
Irish, 131
Ishida, Shunji, Appx
Isolation of design team from French building
    industry, 86–88
Italian, 25, 65, 124, 175
Italian Industry Pavilion (Osaka), 21

Italy, 48, 86

James, Bryn, Appx
Japan, and Japanese, 113, 145, 148
"Jelly-mold scheme, the." *See* APS
Johnson, Philip, 27, 36, 42, 49, 94, [161], 182
Jury report. *See* Competition

Kamiya, Koji, 68
Karelia (Finland), 41
Kawaguchi, 68
Kluver, Billy, 163
Kreutz spherical bearing, 134
Krupp, 69, 113, 114, 119–123, 127, 131, 132,
    Appx

Laclotte, Michel, 27, 38
Lafoucrière, Appx
Lancaster, University of, 47
Language barrier, 65, 86–87
Latin Quarter, 67
Law, Margaret, 138
Lawsuits, 154–155, 169
Leadership, 181
Le Corbusier, 31, 185
Legrand, Bernard, Appx
Lemaret, M., 124
Lenticular screen, 163–164
Libération, 176
Library concept, 2, 174
Library of Beaubourg. *See* BPI
Library of IRCAM, 126
Lichnerowicz, Jacques, Appx
Liebaers, Herman, 38
Lighting, 43, 140, 151, [157], 158, 159, 161, 162,
    163
Lightweight construction, 21, 28
Limestone stratum, 118
Lincoln Center (New York), 9, 10
Linney, Ange, 47
Listener, The, 174
Littlewood, Joan, 25
Lloyd's of London building, 88, 152
Logan, William, Appx
Lohse, Johanna, Appx
Lombard, François, 8, 9, 10, 11, 12, 13, 58, 60, 100,

124, 164, 176, Appx
London, 3, 5, 6, 9, 31, 59, 73, 114, 138, 159
   Crystal Palace, 67, 181, 182
Long life, 148, 180
Loste, Sébastien, 8, 9, 10, Appx
Louvers, 126
Louvre, 38, 48, 50, 53, 172
Lyonnet, Daniel, Appx

MacIntosh, Frazer, Appx
Maintenance, [18], 127, [136], 151, 152, 164, 179
Maintenance cabs, [98], [147]
Maison Carrée (Nîmes), 21
Maison de la Culture, 9, 10
Maison de la Publicité, 32
Malraux (André), 9, 10
Mandolite, 141
Manhole covers, 118
Manufacturers, 29, 87, 95, 129, 130, 143, 146, 148
Marais district, 1, 66
Maranite, 141
Martin, John, 70–71f
Management contractor, 76–78, 85–88
Mathey, François, Appx
May Events of Paris 1968, 3, 4, 26, 67, 74, 180
McNeil, Helen, xiii
Mecca, 8, 29, 67
Mechanical equipment, 80, 93, 132, 144, 145, 146,
   148, 149, 160, 161, 170
   on exterior, x, [18], 25, 26, 31, [120], 125, 126,
     [128], 139, 140, 141, [142], 148, [153]
Mediterranean, 83, 180
Megastructure, 175, 185–186, 185f
Merello, Benedetto, 59, 60, 66
MERO system, 67
Merz, Peter, Appx
Métreur, 70, 76
Mezzanine, 143, 157–158, 162, 163, 180
Milan, 5, 6
Miller, John, 47, 52, 59
Millier, Jean, 176
Mineral fiber, 67, 141
Minister of Production, 113
Ministers of Culture, 93, 124
Mirrors (for lenticular screen), 163
Mixed-use concept, 2, 10, 175–176

Modern art museum of Beaubourg. *See* CNAM
Modernism, 21
Modern movement, 22
Module, 159
Mollard, Claude, 12, Appx
Molybdenum, 122
Moment envelope, 134
Monde, Le, 174
Montmartre, ix
Montreal, 12, 28
Mont-Saint-Michel and Chartres, 187
Monument, and monumentality, 42, 123, 154, 172,
   175, 182, 186, 187
Morale. *See* Staff infighting and morale
Morrison, John, 117
Moscow, 12
Movement, 31, 32, 152
Mullions, [147]
Multi-use space. *See* Forum
Munich, 28, 67, 68, 69
Musée National d'Art Moderne, 2, [184]. *See also*
   CNAM
Music and acoustics institute. *See* IRCAM
"M zero" fire rating, 160

Napoleon, 2
Naruse, Hiroshi, Appx
Nationalities of design team, 168
National Westminster Bank, 66, 169
Navvies, 131
Nehru, Pandit, 21
New Ash Green (London), 65
New Statesman, The, 174, 174f
New York, 3, 9, 175
   Crystal Palace, 67
Nickel, 122
Niemeyer, Oscar, 27
Nippon Steel, 113
Nitzchke, Oscar, 32, 162, 179
Nonprogrammed activities, 101, 104, 162, 163, 179
North Sea, 121. *See also* Ocean drilling platforms
Nôtre-Dame de Paris, ix, 26, 111
Nuclear reactor plants, 88, 121

O'Brien, Turlogh, 138
O'Byrne, Patrick, Appx

Ocean drilling platforms, 88, 181
Offices, professional, 62, 91, 92
Officials, 99
Okabe, Nori (Noriaki), 165, Appx
Olivetti, 5, 20
Olympic Stadium (Munich), 28, 29, 69
Olympic-style scoreboard, 163
Opening of building officially, x, 168, 170
Open plans, 94, 102
Open space under building. *See* Pilotis
Open University (U.K.), 26
Ordre des Architectes, 78
Organization of building, ix
ORTF, 12, 162
Orthographic drawings. *See* Drawings
Osaka, 5, 21, 67, 68
Otis of France, 96–97, 148, Appx
Otto, Frei, 8, 13, 14, 28, 69
Ove Arup and Partners, ix, 5, 19, 27, 28, 29, 30, 41,
    42, 55, 59, 60, 61, 67, 69, 70, 71, 73, 74, 75,
    79, 80, 81, 82, 83, 86, 89, 90, 106, 108, 112,
    122, 125, 126, 129, 132, 132f, 140f, 146,
    165, 170, 183, Appx
  administrative structure of, 7
  Beaubourg fee of (*see* Fees, professional)
  contract for Beaubourg of (*see* Contracts,
    professional)
  design precepts for Beaubourg of, 28–30, 129
  fears of being supplanted of, 60
  formation of, 7–8
  Highways & Bridges Transportation group of, 31
  job administration and staffing of, 93, 114, 115f
  mechanical equipment engineers of, 65, 145, 146
  other research staff of, 138
  professional ("technical") role of, 59–60,
    132–137
  project planning group of, 89, 168
  quantity surveyors of, 75–76, 80–81, 93, 118,
    130, 170
  refusal to sign contract of, 73–75, 114
  relationship with P & R of, 82–83, 90, 169
  staff of, commuting to Paris, 65, 90
  Structures 3 division of, 7, 13, 14, 16, 29, 62,
    114

Palais de Chaillot, 2, 158

Palais-Royal, 164
Pantheon (Rome), 182
Paris
  demonstrations of 1968 (*see* May Events of Paris
    1968)
  École des Beaux-Arts, 71
  as heart of French state, 2
  living in, 63, 64–65, 89 (*see also* France, living
    in)
  Préfect of, 3
  setting up offices in, 54, 90, 92 (*see also* Offices,
    professional)
  Ville de, 155
Parisian culture, 175
Parking, ix, 11, 31, 118, 119
Parliamentary office building (London competition),
    15
Partitions, 159, 165, 180
Pascal, Blaise, 1
Pavement, 164
Paxton, Joseph, 181. *See also* London, Crystal Palace
Pedestrians, 24, 163. *See also* Circulation, pedestrian
Pelli, Cesar, 15f
Performance specification, 122, 130, 146
Penalties in professional contract, 72–73, 81
Penguin Books, 66
Pecquet, Claude, Appx
Perrault, Claude, 53
Perry, Dean and Stewart, 186, 186f
"Petit Beaubourg" (IRCAM), 125, 126
Peutz & Associates, 165
Philadelphia, 41
Philosophy, working, 22
Piano & Rogers, ix, 5, 13, 14, 15, 19, 20, 22, 25,
    37, 38, 40, 41, 47, 51, 52, 55, 59, 60, 62, 63,
    66, 69, 73, 75, 79, 80, 81, 82, 83, 90, 94,
    105, 125, 129, 130, 154, 156, 159, 160, 162,
    165, 170, 179, Appx
  attire of employees of, 53
  Beaubourg contract of (*see* Contracts,
    professional)
  Beaubourg fee of (*see* Fees, professional)
  "coordinator" role of, 63, 91–92
  departure of Su Rogers from, 59
  design precepts for Beaubourg of, 21–22, 27, 129
  facades and galleries team, 92, 143, 149, 158

formation of, 5–7
IRCAM team, 92, 125
job administration and staffing in, 63, 91–93
job (team) leadership, 62–63, 125, 131, 143
learning about winning competition, 37–38
lecture of, to client, 102–105
meeting with Pompidou of, 52–54
planning and furniture team, 92, 149
professional ("creative") role of, 60
relationship with Arup, 82–83, 90, 169
staff working hours, 65
substructure and mechanical equipment team,
    92, 117
superstructure and mechanical equipment team,
    92, 97, 143, 145–150
systems/audiovisuals team, 92, 143, 158
working capital, 66, 75
Piano, Renzo, xiii, 5, 7, 15, 16, 17, 19, 22, 26, 27,
    28, 31, 37, 41, 47, 48, 50, 52, 53, 54, 59,
    62, 64, 65, 66, 74, 83, 86, 92, 94, 101, 124,
    137, 138, 139, 143, 154, [167], 179, 180,
    185, 187, Appx
    design precepts for Beaubourg of, 20–21
    relationship with Rogers of, 64, 66, 166
    joint venture office with Rice of, 66, [167]
Piazza, [viii], ix, [xiv], 4, 25, 26, 31, 32, 33, 63,
    101, 104, [161], 162, 163, 164, 170, 171,
    [172], [178], 179
Pical, 141
Piccadilly Circus, 164
Picon, Gaëtan, 27, 38
Pierce, Rob, 117, Appx
Pilotage, 71, 76
Pilotis, 31, 42, 43, 100, 180
Pipes, 25
Place des Vosges, 66
Plaster, 68
Plateau Beaubourg. See Beaubourg
Plattner, Bernard, 131, Appx
Plumbing equipment, 87, 146, 148, 149, [153]. See
    also Mechanical equipment
Pneumatique. See Inflatable structure
Pohlig, 69, 121, Appx
Police, 67, 137, 138
Polymorphousness, 175, 183
Pont à Mousson, 114, 134

Pompidou, Georges, ix, 2, 3, 8, 9, 10, 11, 47, 55,
    60, 171, 174
    death of, 123, [167], 169
    meeting with, 52–54
Pompidou, Mme, [153], 154, 171
Power supply, 150
Prefabrication, 27, 28, 130, 131, 146, 147
Press coverage, 173–175
Prestige, 29, 88, 151
Price, Cedric, 25
Prince Charles, 187
Private commission, 180
Process of design, xi, 95
Profit margin, 121, 139
Program for the building design, 8–9, 100–101, 125
Program for construction. See Construction,
    timetable
Programmation group. See Client, programmation
    group
Progress checks, 168
Projector and projection screen. See Screen,
    information
Prouvé, Jean, 27, 38, 42, 73, 93, 155
Prudhomme, Jean-Marc, Appx
Public
    attendance, 172, 175
    opinion, 175
    scrutiny, 180
Public halls, ix
Public relations, 123
Pumps, 117

Quality control, 77, 87, 121–122
Quantity production, 27
Quantity surveyors. See Ove Arup and Partners

Rabeneck, Andrew, 175
Randazzo, Vincent, Appx
Rational design, 21, 22
Reading areas, 162
Reception, ix, 104
Recognition of achievement, 83, 180
Rectangular plan, 21
Redundancy, selective, [56], 141, 171
Reference values, 121
Regard, Robert, 12, 38, 41, 54, 79

Replaceability, and replacement, [18], 19, [120],
Replaceability, and replacement (*Continued*)
    [147], 149, 179
Research laboratories, 126
Reliance Controls Factory, 6, 21
Reservoirs (for basement flooding), 117
Restaurant. *See* Cafe
Retaining wall for excavation, 118
Reversibility. *See* Flexibility
RIBA (Royal Institute of British Architects), 13, 16,
    57
Rice, Peter, xiii, 7, 8, 14, 15, 16, 19, 28, 29, 30, 47,
    50, 52, 58, 59, 64, 67, 68, 69, 83, 87, 88, 94,
    95, 112, 115, 115f, 122, 124, 139, 145,
    Appx
    joint venture office of, with Piano, 66
Richardson, Martin, 63
Rigadeau, Gérard, Appx
Riyadh (Saudi Arabia), 8, 29
Rocksil, 141
Rogers, Charles F., 186f
Rogers, Ernesto, 6
Rogers, Richard, xiii, 5, 6, 13, 14, 15, 16, 19, 21,
    22, 27, 28, 31, 32, 36, 37, 41, 47, 48, 49, 52,
    53, 54, 58, 59, 61, 62, 64, 66, 74, 83, 86, 90,
    94, 101, 113, 124, 143, 150, 151, 152, 154,
    155, 162, 171, 174, Appx
    design precepts for Beaubourg of, 20
    relationship with Piano of, 64, 66, 166
Rogers, Ruth (Ruthie), 37, 47, 48, 52, 66
Rogers, Su, 6, 14, 15, 16, 19, 21, 22, 27, 28, 31, 37,
    41, 47, 51, 59, 64, 183
Rohrbach (Germany), 134
Rome, 21, 182
Roof, 127
Royal Institute of British Architects. *See* RIBA
Royal Library of Belgium, 38
Rudolph, Paul, 103
Rue de Renard, 44, [128], 135, 139, 141, 163, 174
Rue Ste. Croix de la Bretonnerie, 66
Rungis, 1
Ruppard, Ken, 165, Appx
Rust, 149

St. Germain, 65
St. Laurent, Yves, 151

Sandberg, Wilhelm, 27, 60, 93
San Diego, 163
Sargent, Michael, 31, Appx
Saridjin, Harry, Appx
Saudi Arabia, 5
Saunier Duval, Appx
Schlegel, Helga, Appx
Schwartz/Silver Architects (Boston), 186f
Screen, information, 162–164, 179, 180
Security, 103, 162, 170, 171
Seguin, Jean-Pierre, Appx
Seine, 48, 92, 111
Self-expression, 154
Scale of building, 29
Scarmagno (Italy), 20
Schulz, Bernard, 11
Services. *See* Mechanical equipment
Ship turbines, 29
Shop drawings, 123, 130, 147
Shutters, rolling, [147]
Signing system. *See* Graphics for Centre
Simplicity, 45, 46, 61, 166, 182
Sircus, Jan, 165, Appx
Site boundary, 154–155
Sitework, 129, 130, 131
Situationists, 4
Silver, Nathan, 174f
Silver, Robert, 186f
Ski lifts, 110
Sluice gates, 29
Social benefits, 26, 104, 125
Social change, 21, 102. *See also* May Events of Paris
    1968
SOCOTEC (insurance authority), 99, 138
Sofitel Bourbon, 51
Solar screening, 143
Sores, Appx
Sound chambers, 126
Soundproofing, 125
South Africa, 115
South Bank (London), 9
Space program, 121, 149
Spans, enormous, 183
Spatial inflation. *See* Building volume
Spatial usability and variations, 102, 180
Specifications, 130, 147

Spielmann, Claudette, Appx

Spontaneity, 183

"Sputnik, The," [84]

Sprinklers, 137, 140, 141, 146

Staff infighting and morale (of design team) 63, 64, 90–91, 92, 114, 166–168, 181

Staff hiring (of design team), 62. *See also* Piano & Rogers *or* Ove Arup and Partners, job administration and staffing

Stainless steel, 152, 154

Stairs, 25, 140, [153]

Standardization, 160

Stanton, Alan, xiii, 60, 62, 63, 143, 150, 151, 152, 158, 162, 163, 183, Appx

Stedelijk Museum (Amsterdam), 27, 60, 93

Steel, 20, 25, 68, 131–137, [133], 148.   *See also* Superstructure

    bidding (tendering) crisis, 112–114, 166, 169

    cast, 28, 29, 67, 68, 108, [116], 121–122, 134–135, [144]

    columns, 30, 106, 132, 133, 134

    diagonal bracing, [18], 32, [56], [84], 134, 135, [142], 171

    economical use of, 61, 81

    fire safety of, 67, 138, 140, 141, [144]

    furniture, 160

    gable frames, [116], 132, 135, [136]

    gerberettes (cantilever beams), [84], 106, [107], 108, [111], 133, 134, [136], 140, [147], 171

    metallurgy, 29, 68, 108, 121–122, [144], 166

    "primary," [34], 123, 143, 158, 166

    rolled, 29, 68

    "secondary," 144

    specification crisis, 121–122, 166, 169

    technology, 29, 67, 68

    tension ties, 30, 131, 132, 134, 135

    "tertiary," [34], 141, 141f, 144, 145

    truss girders, 30, 108, [109], 131, 132, 135, 154, 183, [184]

    Vierendeel trusses, 61, 106

    Warren trusses, 106

    weight of, 135

Steel construction. *See* Structure of building

Steel pressure vessels, 121

Stone, Denis, 76, Appx

Stoved (baked) finishes, 141, 149, 160

Strafor, 159

Street theater, 25

Strength (of steel), 122

Stringer, George, 57–58

Structural Engineer, The, 71f

Structure of building, x, 81, 85, 149, 152, 170, 183. *See also* Substructure

    assembly of, [111], 131–132, 137 (*see also* Construction, delivery, assembly, and erection)

    bays of, 132, 157, 158

    floors of, 132, 135, 141, 144

    space frame of, 28, 67

    steel castings of, 28, 29, 67, 120–122 (*see also* Steel)

    structural cage/frame of, 32, 132, 151, 156–157, 180 (*see also* Superstructure)

Studios, electro-acoustic, 126

Style, 187–188

Subcontracts, 80, 130, 159. *See also* Contractors

Subliming paint. *See* Building finishes

Substructure, 80, 90, 92, 117, 119, 123, 130, [172]. *See also* Structure of building

Success of Beaubourg, 176, 179. *See also* Design of Beaubourg, critical appreciation; Public opinion

Sunday Telegraph, The, 174

Sunday Times, The, 174

Supergraphics, [128], 163

Superstructure, 80, 87, 92, 117, 118, 127, 131–137, [133]. *See also* Structure of building

Suppliers. *See* Manufacturers

Swedish, 124

Swindon (U.K.), 21

Swiss, 117

Sydney Opera House, 5, 8, 28, 29, 74, 74f, 80, 90

Tailhardat, Pierre, Appx

Takahashi, Hiroyuki, Appx

Tange, Kenzo, 67, 68

Team 4, 6

Technical control systems, 162

Technology

    advanced, 28, 31, 87, 95, 108, 131, 149, 150, 181, 185

    musical, 126

Technology *(Continued)*
  nineteenth-century, 29, 67, 181
  rational choices of, 181–182
  resources of, 102, 118
  trust in, 21, 27, 187
Temperature changes, 149, 162
Tempering (of steel), 122
Temporary exhibit areas, x
"Termite creativity," 148, 150
Terraces, exterior, x, 32, [109], [144], 171
Thaury, Jean, 87, Appx
Theft from Centre, 179
Thermolag, 149
Times, The, 174
Times Square, 162
Timetable. *See* Construction, timetable
Titanium, 122
Tivoli Gardens, 162
Toilets, 11, 141, 143, 177
Total cost. *See* Construction, final costs
Tourists, 172
Tokyo, 67
Trafalgar Square, 36
Traffic
  basement links to, 31
  road, 26, [128]
Translator. *See* Interpreter
Tripes. *See* "Guts"

United States, 28, 121, 187
Universal Oil Products, 6
Uplift (hydraulic force), 117, 118, 119
Utzon, Jorn, 27, 38, 74, 74f, 103

Valensi, Colette, Appx
Value for money. *See* Cost-effectiveness
Vanifibre, 141
Vaniscotte, Michel, Appx
VDA (graphic designers), 177
Ventilation equipment, 120, 145, 146, [153]
Venturi, Robert, 41
Verbizh, Rainer, Appx
Vermiculite cement, 141
Viatte, Germain, 11, Appx
Victorian recreation piers, 110
Viipuri Library (Finnish Karelia), 41

Vienna, 14f
Visitors to Centre. *See* Public, attendance
Vitality, 185
Voyer, Appx

Wannifibre, 141
Washington D.C., 3
Wasted expense, 123
Water, 145, 148, 149, 152
Water tanks, 139
Waterproofing, 119
Watt, Brian, 70–71f, 74, 112, 115, 115f
Weather damage, and weather resistance, [18],
  148–149
Weeks, Russell, 41
Welding, 108, 131, 135
Wellesley College Science Center, 186, 186f
Wilson, Colin St. John, 27
Wind and stability loads, 133–135
Wind problems, 180
Wolff Olins, 13
Wood, 160
Workers, 131, 170
Working drawings. *See* Architectural plans kept
  fluid; Competition submission; Drawings
Wrought iron, 25, 68

Yale School of Architecture, 6, 27, 32
Young, John, 6, 16, 19, 31, 38, 41, 47, 48, 49, 52,
  53, 59, 60, 63, 149, 159, Appx

Zbinden, Walter, 117, Appx
"Zip-up" buildings, 6, 21